D1528439

Never too old to backpack

More Algarve hiking

Tracy Burton

DEDICATION

To my late parents Elizabeth Ann and Thomas George Burton who encouraged me to walk everywhere as a child and ignited my lifelong love of hiking..

CONTENTS

vi

DAILY DISTANCES

Link routes

The routes we walked are:

- Loulé to Salir/Salir to Loulé: 56.4km (full distance)
- Mexilhoeira Grande to Monchique: 25.4km
- Marmelete to Aljezur: 18.6km

The ones we didn't walk are:

- Parises to São Brás de Alportel: 18.4km
- Lagos to Bensafrim: 10.1km
- Albufeira to Alte: 29km

Alternative finish via Aljezur and the Rota Vicentina (GR11)

- Aljezur to Arrifana: 12km
- Arrifana to Carrapateira: 24km
- Carrapateira to Vila do Bispo: 22km
- Vila do Bispo to Cabo de São Vicente: 14km

INTRODUCTION

When we waved goodbye to Portugal after completing the Via Algarviana in May 2015, we certainly didn't expect to be returning to Algarve just six months later. A major UK outdoor publisher had initially expressed an interest in Harri's proposed guidebook to the 300-kilometre trail across Portugal's southernmost region but, when they failed to respond to numerous follow-up emails, we concluded they were no longer interested.

We had no real need to return to Algarve that autumn, and yet the lure of southern Portugal was just too strong to resist. Moreover, having barely lifted our heads from our computer screens all summer, we were in desperate need of stretching (and tanning) our legs.

The sooner we could get away the better; however, any October travel plans needed to sit neatly between two dates. I was running the Cardiff Half Marathon at the beginning of the month and Harri was honour-bound to fulfil a long-arranged walking guide engagement in the middle. We were looking for eleven days of good hiking in a warm climate. But while our heads were insisting it was time to venture somewhere new, our hearts refused to listen: there was only one place we wanted to hike and it was Algarve.

Harri checked the average temperatures in Algarve for early to mid-October, while I looked into flights to Faro from Bristol airport. There was one big difference this time around: we would be leaving our camping gear behind. We'd had little difficulty securing good value accommodation when we'd been hiking east to west across inland Algarve (apart from an unforgettable night in Marmelete), so it seemed crazy to lug around a tent and the associated paraphernalia *just in case*. Harri was delighted because it meant him carrying a lighter load, and I did a little jig of happiness because I have hated camping ever since (or perhaps as a result of) my Brownie days.

We looked forward to again exploring an Algarve of sleepy, unspoilt villages, rolling hills, dry orchards and cork forests – a place where life hasn't changed much in decades.

Day after day in May, our eyes had feasted on the spectacular landscape, tranquil except for the birdsong and hum of bees. We'd passed through depopulated villages, witnessed disused water mills and long-abandoned agricultural terraces, and followed for hours the snaking shoreline and turquoise waters of the Barragem do Arade.

While the landscape was stunning, hiking across Algarve had been surprisingly tough and more challenging than we'd anticipated, with undulating trails, steep climbs and long days. The unusually high temperatures made the walking harder still, and we got terrifyingly close to dehydration when we ran out of water on one long section.

In traditional villages like Furnazinhas, Cachopo, Barranco de Velho and Salir, we dined and wined like kings. Speaking little Portuguese, we often struggled to make ourselves understood; however, we were treated with unbelievable kindness by our gracious Portuguese hosts, who would often phone ahead to ensure we had a bed for the following night.

This time around, we would not be following one linear trail, but walking several of the six 'link' routes which connect various points on the Via Algarviana with local towns and, in the case of Albufeira and Lagos, the coast.

After completing one of those link routes (Marmelete to Aljezur), Harri wanted us to check out an alternative, mostly coastal finish from Aljezur to Cabo de São Vicente along the Trilho dos Pescadores (Fishermen's Trail) and Rota Vicentina.

Postscript:

After months of silence, we returned from this trip to limited good news. The publisher was very interested in Harri's proposal, on the proviso that the publication date might be up to two years in the future. After much consideration, Harri decided to thank them for their interest, but turn them down and self-publish *The Via Algarviana: an English guide to the 'Algarve Way'* as an ebook.

For photographs visit <u>uk.pinterest.com/thewalkerswife</u>

THE VIA ALGARVIANA

It was an Englishman – the late Maurice Clyde – who came up with the idea for a scenic walking trail between Alcoutim and Portugal's most south-westerly point at Cabo de São Vicente.

The Loulé-based environmental group Almargem was enthusiastic from the outset and the project was immediately named the Via Algarviana (although Maurice and the other Brits tended to refer to it as the 'Algarve Way'). While Almargem set about securing funding, Maurice and his hiking friends began to establish the route on the ground.

Between 1997 and 1999, Maurice and his British walking friends, members of Os Caminheiros do Algarve Walkers, completed first the section between São Bartolomeu de Messines to the Cabo de São Vicente and subsequently the entire route.

In 2001, Almargem and Maurice's walking group organised a symbolic opening of the section of route between Alte and São Bartolomeu de Messines. Sadly, in 2002 a major stroke ended Maurice's personal involvement with his beloved project; it was left to Almargem to take the project forward.

The present-day Via Algarviana reflects the experiences and suggestions of many seasoned Algarve hikers. The main difference between the original route and the Almargem trail is that Maurice's route joined the west coast soon after Marmelete, whereas the present-day Via Algarviana (the route we walked) remains inland until the final day's walking between Vila do Bispo and Cabo de São Vicente.

To avoid potential future conflict with land owners, the 300-kilometre trail sticks to public access paths wherever possible, while avoiding proper roads and pavements (except in towns and villages). This means that in places, the official route lacks the scenic quality of the tracks and paths known and walked by local people.

The route meanders through the Algarve from east to west (or *vice versa*), passing through eleven municipalities – Alcoutim, Aljezur, Castro Marim, Tavira, São Brás de Alportel, Loulé, Silves, Monchique,

Lagos, Portimão and Vila do Bispo – with the most rural villages being found in the east.

Some of the strange directional convolutions, like Alcoutim to Balurcos or São Bartolomeu de Messines to Silves, arise from an attempt to align the trail with facilities and accommodation (thus benefiting both the hiker and the local economy).

The Via Algarviana has now been designated GR13 (a *Grande Rota* (GR) is an official European long-distance path) and it is waymarked accordingly. It is promoted as a two-week route with fourteen sections of varying length; however, some hiking companies offer shorter options, for example, one week's hiking from Alte to Cabo de São Vicente.

For photographs visit uk.pinterest.com/thewalkerswife

ARRIVING IN ALGARVE

It's no exaggeration to say that Google Street View has transformed our hiking life.

For those who are not already enamoured with this astonishing technology, Street View enables people to get 360-degree views of the majority of roads and urban areas in the UK (and much of the world – though it has been banned in some countries, like India, and has never been re-introduced in Austria after privacy concerns led to a one-year ban being imposed in May 2010). Street View means you can take a virtual stroll around almost any part of a country that takes your fancy and get a close-up view of local buildings and landmarks ... though not people and licence plates as these are deliberately blurred.

Of course, you could argue that half the fun of visiting a town, city or village for the first time is having no idea what the streets and houses will look like, and that Google Street View has to some extent taken away the thrill of arriving someplace new.

Harri disagrees, believing that forewarned is forearmed. Nowadays, long before we roll into a new town, he'll have checked it out online, with the result that every pavement, street corner, yellow line and lamp-post is as familiar as his cornflake bowl. Harri uses Google Street View to identify footpaths zigzagging through housing estates and to locate unobtrusive places for us to park without paying. When we are using old hiking guides, he double-checks that no recent developments – housing, a new retail park – are likely to hinder our progress, and looks for pubs along our route.

In fact, Harri now uses Google Street View (in conjunction with Strava and Viewranger) to plan our European hikes, which is how he found out that it was perfectly possible to walk from Faro airport to the city's railway station – thus saving the €10 taxi fare. I had my reservations, mostly because walking from (or even to) airports isn't something you hear about people doing. For starters, the road systems around airports are notoriously complicated, as highlighted by the constant stream of hire car drivers circling the vicinity slowly and methodically in their desperate efforts to *get out*. Otherwise, the traffic is mostly comprised of taxis, which have an unnerving tendency to swerve into the kerb you've just stepped off, slamming on their brakes just as your life flashes in front of your eyes.

Harri's idea of walking from Faro airport originated from an article written by the English author Will Self (coincidentally just three months younger than me, though in possession of much longer legs). Like us, Will Self likes walking ... a lot ... and he frequently takes himself off for epic walks. It was while visiting the US that he decided to walk from New York's Kennedy Airport to Manhattan. As anyone who has ever tried to walk in the US – other than along waymarked trails in National and State Parks – will tell you, it is not a pedestrian-friendly country. In the States, the automobile rules – the only people who walk are those who can't afford alternative transport.

This curious national resistance to walking anywhere is reflected in America's infrastructure, meaning that even when you do want to walk it's damned near impossible. I was once reduced to jet-lagged tears when, after deciding to walk the relatively short distance from San Diego's Old Town to Hotel Circle, my youngest daughter and I found the route ahead intersected by an almighty road. We could see our hotel over there, on the far side of the Mission Valley Freeway, but we just couldn't work out how to get under/over/across that thunderous barrier on foot.

My experiences in the States mean I have the utmost respect for Will Self, not only for trying, but for succeeding in arriving in Manhattan on foot and in one piece. Even so, his trek wasn't all plain sailing; at one point, the road he was following temporarily ran out of sidewalk. Self stopped a passerby for advice, as you would, and was astonished to hear the other man insist that Manhattan could only be reached on wheels. Self later recounted how the American 'couldn't conceptually grasp the idea of walking to New York'.

Thankfully, Harri's proposed airport walk was nothing like the magnitude of Will Self's New York expedition. Faro's railway station was just a ten-kilometre stroll away and the majority of the route was traffic-free. Our biggest challenge was working out how to get out of the airport. Predictably, there were no signs stating 'pedestrians this way' (or the Portuguese equivalent) and there was plenty of the anticipated hire car dodging before we finally exited the airport and set off along the single level track that Harri had spotted during his online 'meander' around the lagoon.

We easily located the dusty track which led us around the furthermost reaches of the Rio Formosa and delivered us to the Ecovia do Litoral, a 'continuous' 214-kilometre cycle path running along Algarve's coastline. (Although the continuous claim is somewhat dubious as we found out when we attempted to walk from Olhão to Faro on a subsequent trip. The path was great for the first few miles, but the Ecovia waymarks ended abruptly west of Olhão, after which we found ourselves walking miles along the hard shoulder of the busy N125.)

There was fine rain in the air as we strolled among tall bamboo canes interspersed with traditional housing and modern villas. For the first few kilometres, the sudden roar of an engine every five minutes or so served as a constant reminder of the airport's proximity, until eventually the noise faded into the distance and we could concentrate on the sounds of the surrounding landscape.

Having arrived in the upmarket district of Montenegro without any problem, we were now somewhat confused. A waymark indicated that the cycle path continued to our right, running parallel to the single track railway – the Linha do Algarve – that links Lagos in the west to Vila Real de Santo António on the Spanish border. Except, here on the ground, the cycle path didn't appear to continue to anywhere ... not only was there was a wide dry ditch to circumnavigate, but the track immediately beyond was blocked off by high fencing.

I glanced at Harri. His pained expression denoted his deep sense of betrayal. He stared into the distance, his earlier confidence that we could reach Faro station by foot fast fading. I guessed what he was thinking: *how could Google Street View do this to me?*

We were standing there, uncertain what to do, wondering what Will Self would do, when a man on a bike rolled up. Recognising our bewilderment, he kindly stopped and in faltering English explained that we needed to walk along the actual railway track for a short distance. Only after we had passed the dilapidated house alongside the railway line, he said, would we be able to join the cycle path again.

We later learned the reason behind the hiatus in the *ecovia*: the owner of the property and the 12,000m^2 of surrounding land was in a bitter battle with the authorities over the price he should receive for his land.

The impassable ditch and an iron grid were just some of the physical obstacles he had employed in his determination to derail the Parque Ribeirinho de Faro project, while decrying the claim of the Portuguese Environment Agency that the disputed land was in the Maritime Public Domain, i.e. it should not be occupied but preserved and kept free for public use.

It looked like a brief stroll along the railway track was unavoidable if we weren't to miss our train; however, it was with some relief that we clambered down the embankment on the far side of the fence and rejoined the cycle path.

(NB We are uncertain how the issue was resolved in the end – we think the land in question was legally declared to be public land – but when we revisited Faro again in 2017, the fencing had gone and the cycle path was at last passable.)

Like many historic ports, Faro's waterfront had been in decline for many years, with empty, ruined warehouses and tide mills, relics of centuries of salt gathering. The idea behind the creation of Parque Ribeirinho de Faro was to link the two distinct parts of Faro, i.e. the city to the east of the railway station and the salty waters of the Rio Formosa lagoon on the far side of the track.

The *parque* opened in 2014 and covers around 16 hectares. There is a small open amphitheatre for outdoor entertainment, a children's playground and an exercise trail. As we witnessed ourselves, the predominantly traffic-free landscape is extremely popular with runners, dog walkers and anyone who simply enjoys a nice, flat walk in pleasant surroundings.

Faro's old station was unchanged since our last visit. We toyed briefly with the idea of wandering into the old town to kill the hour or so until our train departed and had actually walked a short distance when Harri recalled how, on our last visit, Faro's labyrinth of historic, narrow streets had been filled with cats ... indolent felines stretching out in the sun like artists' models. Once the latent photographer in me was awakened, who knew how long I'd spend snapping away.

There was the very real danger of us missing our train if we lost track of the time, so we reluctantly headed back to the station, where we settled ourselves down in the familiar bar with its tree growing

9

through the roof, sipping cold beer and gazing outside with sinking hearts as the rain grew heavier. We'd come to Algarve looking for sunshine but right now the sky looked about as promising as the one we'd left behind in Bristol.

In the run-up to our trip, I'd spent some time honing my Portuguese language skills with the excellent Duo Lingo and having achieved 11% Portuguese fluency I was keen to practice my skills at the bar. It was some time later that I realised I'd been learning Brazilian Portuguese and its somewhat different pronunciation.

'*Dois cervajas, por favour,*' I said confidently. The barmaid nodded, indicating there was a choice: draught or bottled lager. Unfortunately, 'bottle' falls into the 89% of Portuguese I wasn't yet fluent in, so I pointed towards the shelf with a smile. When I went to the bar for the second time – we had a long wait for our train– I discovered the barmaid was at least 70% fluent in English.

When we walked the Via Algarviana, we'd caught the train from Faro to Vila Real de Santo António. The journey took just over an hour and I was so exhausted from lack of sleep the previous night I could barely keep my eyes open. This time we were heading west to Loulé, I was wide awake having managed a full six hours sleep before the alarm went off at 2.45am, and our journey would take just 16 minutes.

Now Harri has a tendency to keep things vague when he knows the detail would a) annoy, b) worry, or c) confuse me. I'm not certain which response he was anticipating – maybe a combination of all three – however, in no prior discussion did he mention that Loulé station is not actually in Loulé at all. Of course, seven and a half kilometres is no distance at all by car. Drivers covering the journey in ten minutes likely have no idea that the most direct *walking* route between Loulé's station and the city itself involves steady climbing, the careful navigation of a steep and undulating stretch of undergrowth below the A22 (Algarve's principal motorway) and a final drag up to the city. Loulé station, I learned as I stepped off the train, is actually located in Quatro Estradas and isn't actually in Loulé at all.

The weather was still refusing to behave in an Algarvian manner and I was feeling rather downhearted when we rolled up at the Loulé Jardim Hotel. This charming hotel with its lush, inner courtyard, incredible spiral staircase and panoramic views across the city was just what we needed to lift our spirits (even if it wasn't quite warm enough to use the rooftop pool).

Our unusually shaped room was large and airy, and the elegant furnishings and tasteful decor included pale grey ceilings, which believe me look far better than they sound. For once I was glad of the bath – Cardiff's road surfaces are hard and unforgiving on the feet. At the end of the race, it had been my left foot giving me grief, now it seemed my aches and pains had switched to my right one. I hoped this was not a bad omen because the last thing I wanted was to be hobbling across Algarve.

Trying to ignore my aching feet and the grey skies, we set off to explore the beautiful market town of Loulé. The origins of the city are disputed, with some historians believing it dates back to the Carthageans, and others the Romans. Whatever the truth, the city became more important under the rule of the Moors from the 8th to 13th centuries.

Like the castle at nearby Salir, Loulé's Moorish castle was constructed from stone and 'taipa' (a mixture of mud and sandstone) and the area contained within the castle walls was roughly twelve acres. The town was conquered by Dom Afonso III in 1249 and the Moors moved outside this inner area to quarters outside the city walls known as *mourarias*.

Loulé continued to develop, particularly after 1291, when King Dinis introduced Algarve's first medieval fair and it became an important regional trading centre. Now, the narrow, historic streets around the restored castle walls and tower are dominated by traffic and it was impossible to take a decent close-up photograph, let alone imagine medieval traders setting up their stalls.

Loulé has one more claim to fame – Algarve's first hospital was built here in the 15th century to care for soldiers who had been wounded in Portugal's North African campaigns.

Fortunately, we didn't have to worry about wounded soldiers or conquering Christians, just our rumbling tummies. All we wanted was something to eat, followed by an early night; however, it was early and the local restaurants had yet to open their doors for evening service.

We wandered through the quiet streets, stopping to marvel at the cork products being sold in shops – slippers, handbags, wallets, purses, jewellery, even aprons. I'd have loved to have wandered inside and bought something; however, I realised it would be daft to overburden myself on day one. Not that cork is heavy – over 50% of its volume is air – but anything I bought would take up valuable rucksack space and was at risk of getting damaged over the course of nine days' hiking.

It was the Romans who first recognised cork's buoyancy, insulation and shock absorbing properties, using it for the soles of their sandals, to make beehives and to insulate homes. When I was growing up in the seventies not everyone had central heating (we didn't) and I can remember how people often stuck cork tiles to the inside of outside walls in an attempt to retain warmth (cork has low conductivity to heat, noise and vibration and is fire resistant).

We walked the Via Algarviana in a sizzling spring heatwave and when the online guidebook mentioned cork oak 'forests' ahead, we'd naturally thought we were approaching some much-needed respite from the relentless sunshine. Unfortunately, the accepted Portuguese definition of a 'forest' seems to be a scattering of trees on a parched hillside and there was no shade!

Portugal has around 720,000 hectares of cork forest providing about 50% of the world's cork and these stripped, rust-coloured trunks became a familiar sight on the trail. In fact, the cork oak is so important to the country's economy that a law was passed making it illegal for anyone to cut down a cork tree without permission from Portugal's government. If caught doing so, a large fine is imposed, but there is also a non-monetary and more formidable punishment: the landowner is not allowed to use the land for 25 years.

It was still only 6.30pm but there's only so much cork gazing you can do. We wandered past a line of pretty street fountains, where for once Harri resisted the impulse to run straight down the middle, and retraced our steps to a restaurant we'd spotted earlier, set off the street with a pretty courtyard. A pale grey cat, drinking from the narrow water channel running off the Bicas Velhas fountain, barely raised its head as we ambled past. The fountain was completed in 1887 and its four spouts supplied water to the townsfolk and their animals, rarely drying up however hot the weather.

When we got there, our hearts sank – our chosen restaurant wasn't yet open for business. Thankfully, the owner spotted us standing on the pavement looking exhausted and she insisted we go inside to wait. Too tired to do much except flop on the comfortable sofa, we ordered drinks and chatted to an elderly poodle whose fixated stare suggested she found two weary Welsh hikers at least as fascinating as many humans find their dogs.

For photographs visit <u>uk.pinterest.com/thewalkerswife</u>

DAY 1: LOULÉ TO SALIR

One thing Harri hates is having to repeat himself, so when he outlined our hiking itinerary in great detail, I was careful to jot everything down in my diary – the link routes we would be walking, where and when we'd be joining the Rota Vicentina and where we'd be staying each night. By doing this, I reasoned, I wouldn't irritate him by constantly asking about each day's plans. The trouble was, I was now backpacking in Algarve and my diary was lying on my desk at home in South Wales. So where exactly were we heading today?

Salir, he reminded me, we were walking to Salir, a place we'd visited last time around and absolutely adored. Then, tomorrow we would be retracing our steps to Loulé and spending a second night at the delightful Loulé Jardim Hotel. He explained how the 28.2-kilometre waymarked link route from Salir connected the Via Algarviana with Loulé railway station; however, because we'd walked from the station yesterday and were staying in Loulé itself again tomorrow night, we could knock off roughly 15 kilometres meaning we had just over 40 kilometres to cover in two days, a piffling distance for two seasoned backpackers. Wait, I nearly forgot the extra four kilometres we had to cover from (and back to) Fonte Morena, the site of one of many of the area's natural fountains and the spot where the waymarked route to/from Salir begins and ends. So nearly 50 kilometres in total, maybe not such a piffling distance when you consider the terrain was mostly undulating trail and forestry tracks.

We rarely follow out and back routes anymore, having grown tired of the constant need to retrace our steps when we were hiking the Cambrian Way in Wales and needed to get back to our car and tent every evening. These days, we prefer to stick to circular walks so that the landscape around us changes and there's none of the dread that comes with knowing you have to revisit the less enjoyable sections of the route. Sometimes, though, out and back is unavoidable and I had no objection to following this particular linear route because it meant an overnight stop at the enchanting Casa da Mãe. There was also the fried chicken and espatadas at the Papa Gaio Dourado restaurant to look forward to. I think it's fair to say we were both looking forward to returning to Salir.

Fortunately, the weather seemed a lot brighter this morning. Venturing out onto our terrace, I gazed across terracotta tiles and enchanting high-level living spaces towards the distant ocean. As I turned, my eyes were drawn to a white, dome-shaped building perched on a distant hill. I'd noticed it last night, but this morning it looked more striking than ever. Although its distinctive shape brought to mind a mosque what I was looking at was the modern extension of the Nossa Senhora da Piedade, a sixteenth-century Catholic chapel built on a busy Roman route running between São Brás de Alportel, Loulé and Boliqueime.

The original chapel was yet another casualty of the 1755 earthquake; however, it was quickly rebuilt, only to be later dwarfed by the spaceship-like dome which was now capturing my attention.

Breakfast at the Loulé Jardim Hotel was a surprisingly lavish affair, with all sorts of unlikely foods laid out for we guests to gorge on. There's a first for everything, and I'm pretty certain I'd never before seen a whole gateau on a breakfast table before. I felt like a child in a sweetshop, gazing at all that delicious food. Even though I knew I would feel sick if I tried to sample everything, it was very hard to resist piling my plate high. And the infuriating voice of reason was already adding up the calories, cautioning me about bloating and reminding me that outgrowing my hiking shorts at this stage of our trip was not an option.

So I did what anyone confronted with metre after metre of gastronomic delights would do ... I demanded my inner voice shut up and got stuck in. The variety of food on offer was frankly quite incredible. Aside from the usual continental offerings, there was bacon, fried eggs, scrambled eggs, sausage and mushrooms, cream-filled cake, dried figs (which I mistook for chestnuts), pomegranate seeds (which I tried for the first time in decades and loved) and lots of delicious yoghurts. Loulé Jardim Hotel is definitely not the place to stay if you're dieting. You could stick to figs I suppose, but where's the fun in that?

Talking of local produce, we were astonished that pomegranates – around £1 each in supermarkets at home – grow in such abundance here that many are not even harvested but left to rot. Yesterday, we saw over-ripe fruit splitting open on the trees or left decaying on the ground. When we were kids, the availability of fruit and vegetables tended to be seasonal, with pomegranates generally appearing in the shops in the run-up to Halloween. I remember how my younger sister would tuck into them with relish, carefully plucking out the seeds one by one with a large safety pin. The whole process was far too fiddly and time-consuming for my impatient nature so I stuck to apples.

Not wanting to appear greedy, my approach to this morning's unexpected feast was to return to the buffet several times. On one of my repeat visits, I found myself chatting to a fellow guest. Monika hailed from Poland and was travelling alone. There's nothing worse than eating in a dining room or restaurant alone so I invited her to join us.

We learned Monika was an aspiring amateur photographer who had chosen to holiday alone so that she could linger as long as necessary to take the perfect shot. She had chosen Loulé for its central location in Algarve, not realising the city's railway station would be so inconveniently located for the sightseeing trips she had planned. I was glad Harri was able reassure her that the local bus service was good and cheap and she would not have to abandon her plans.

Ever since we'd decided to come here to Loulé, we'd been agonising over the pronunciation of the city's name. To a person, the Brits we had encountered referred to it as Loo-lay, but it felt somewhat improper to echo a word with such scatological connotations. Personally, we were more inclined to think it was Low-laay. Crucially, the emphasis was not on the penultimate syllable but on the accented 'e'. The jury was still out but, until we were told differently, we were sticking to Low-laay.

With few anticipated distractions – or even a bar – on route, Harri was confident we'd cover the distance to Salir in good time. This meant we had time to visit Loulé's splendid municipal market. It was all locked up last night, but this morning it was bustling with local shoppers and tourists alike. The original plans for this remarkable Art Nouveau building with its cream facade and cerise towers were drawn up in the late 19th century by the architect Alfredo Campos; however, the majority of construction work was undertaken in the first decade of the twentieth century when it became the biggest and grandest building project in the municipality.

Unfortunately, the plans for four entrances and four halls were so big and so grand that this imposing neo-Arab building which was meant to symbolise the wealth of the municipality was at risk of bankrupting it! The plans were amended, some of the shops were lost and only two towers were built. Even so, Loulé's market is pretty magnificent by anyone's standards and it has dominated the centre of the city since it opened in 1908.

As we approached from the main street, Harri warned me that anything I felt compelled to buy would be going into *my* rucksack. Not his, mine. Under no circumstances was he carrying a large ceramic dish across the Algarve's hinterland. Did I understand? He was right to be worried.

From the moment we entered the market and glimpsed the colourful displays of edible and non-edible items, I was smitten. Everything looked and smelled so good. It was difficult to resist the urge to scoop up handfuls of olives, nuts and luscious fruit, to ignore the gorgeous earthenware and cork products being offered at such low prices.

There were countless stalls selling piri piri sauce, the pungent chilli and pepper sauce which originated here in Portugal. You'd be hard-pushed to find a restaurant in Algarve which doesn't have chicken piri piri on its menu, but as I'd discovered when walking the Via Algarviana, not all piri piri is equal. Words to the wise here ... add the sauce little by little or you're at risk of blurting out expletives as the fiery flavour hits your taste buds. I guessed the tiny bottles were meant for singletons or households – like ours – where only one of us likes hot food and the larger bottles for die-hard chilli enthusiasts.

The tomatoes piled on the market stalls were as big as grapefruit and reminded me of our last shop in Alcoutim before setting out on the Via Algarviana when I'd bought one and munched it like an apple as we strolled out of town. No-one in Portugal has to campaign for wonky vegetables, they are on display in all their glory at local markets.

I forced myself to ignore the rows of delicious-sounding liquors, knowing I would regret my impulse buying later when I was struggling up a mountain track in the midday heat. My willpower was sorely tested, however, when I spotted bottles of port on offer for €4.85. I looked at Harri, but he shook his head sternly. Not his rucksack, *mine*.

Having been intrigued by the shop windows of cork products last night, it was fascinating to study them up close. Aprons, wallets, purses, keyrings ... I had no idea how they sculpted the cork but the items looked sturdy enough to me. It was October, perhaps time to start thinking about some Christmas shopping. I could think of a few recipients for the cork slippers priced at €30. Harri guessed what I was thinking and his eyes said it all. Not my rucksack, *yours*.

With great reluctance, I turned my back on port, cork slippers and thyme-flavoured honey and headed towards the fresh product stalls. This was why we'd come into the market after all: to purchase fresh supplies for the day. We generally keep it simple when we're walking; bread, cheese, fruit and crisps is ample for our needs, especially when we have a hearty Portuguese evening meal to look forward to.

If we'd been concerned about our lack of Portuguese, we needn't have been. No sooner had a local lady seen us struggling to order some goat's cheese than she took it upon herself to become our personal shopper. This charming lady, who was probably in her seventies, escorted us from stall to stall while we made our meagre purchases of cheese, bread and fruit. The total bill came to just €2.05, which made us look embarrassingly tight when there were so many delicious and delightful wares on offer and local people were spending so freely. Unhappily, it always comes back to weight and whether anything we buy will survive two weeks of being jostled around in a rucksack. Few things tick both boxes.

Our shopping completed, we had one final call to make before leaving Loulé. The Turismo de Algarve publishes a series of very informative leaflets, one about each of the eleven municipalities which comprise the region. Costing just 50 cents each, they include information about the towns and villages, local attractions, a simple map of the area and a street map of the municipality's main commercial centre. We'd bought several maps last time we were here; however, Loulé was missing from our collection.

We headed to the tourist information office on Rua José Viegas Gregório where we made our purchase and got chatting to the assistant. We were amazed to learn that she'd never heard of Casa da Mãe. How could that be, we wondered? Salir was mere minutes away by car and yet, by this lady's own admission, she was not remotely aware of this loveliest of traditional hotels. This dreadful state of affairs had to be rectified, we decided.

Time was passing and we had a long day's hiking ahead of us. First, we had to work out how to actually leave Loulé, because there was no sign of the now-familiar red and white stripes. Fortunately, Harri has been blessed with a remarkable internal compass. He's not unlike a homing pigeon and instinctively seems to know which way we should be heading, even when I haven't got the remotest clue.

On the city outskirts, we were surprised to find ourselves walking alongside a rugby pitch. Several visits to Portugal (and even more to Madeira) have left us in little doubt that football is a national obsession here. But rugby? I didn't even realise the Portuguese played the game. A little online research revealed that Loulé Rugby Club was founded in 1982, replacing the Loulé Rugby Centre which was set up in 1975.

The team quickly adopted a sort of Portuguese *haka* which is sung at the beginning of games at all levels. Google obligingly translates the song title as 'Bring There There' and if you think that sounds unpromising the majority of the song's lyrics are comprised of those same two words – 'bring' and 'there' – with a little bit of counting at the end. The lyrics certainly won't terrify the opposition as much as the All Blacks' cries of 'It is death, it is death', but they don't seem overly inspiring for Loulé's players either.

From the early days, Loulé boosted a women's team, though the lack of competition proved a problem for a while; fortunately, times have changed and today female rugby players are once again out there on the field. When the current rugby field was created, it meant international teams could now be invited to play. First to arrive was the English team, followed by Wales in June 1990 and Ireland in December of the same year. Three decades later, Loulé's enthusiasm for rugby is just as strong. In 2012/13 they moved into the First Division of the Campeonato Nacional de Rugby (National Championship).

After the rugby pitch, there was a skate park and then we were climbing out of Loulé, passing ever more luxurious villas and turning occasionally to look back over the city and the ocean beyond. Occasionally, the sun would burst out from the clouds and we'd enjoy a short spell of sunshine, but it was mostly grey. Having anticipated glorious weather, it was hard not to feel glum when faced with the reality.

After about two hours' walking, we spotted a sign for a café. It meant leaving the waymarked route and heading downhill for a short distance but was almost noon and we figured the sun – if we could actually see it – would be over the yardarm by now.

I'd never heard of a yardarm until I met Harri and, with him being of farming stock, I just assumed it was an old farming expression. Not so! Yardarms were the timbers on the mast of sailing ships from which the square sails were hung. When the sun was high enough in the sky to be visible over the top of the yardarm – around eleven o'clock in summer – the north Atlantic sailors would be allowed their first rum of the day. We take care never to have that first beer until we are certain the captain would allow us our rum.

I think it's fair to say I take after my late mother in having absolutely no sense of direction. It was a running joke in our family that Mam could head into the ladies toilets and emerge minutes later having forgotten where it was she'd left Dad and the rest of us waiting. Always a fast walker despite her diminutive size, she'd stride off purposefully in completely the wrong direction, while we'd be shouting at her to come back.

Mam got equally disorientated in department stores, particularly when escalators and lifts were involved. On one unforgettable shopping trip to Cardiff, I spent almost an hour hunting for her in bhs, only to eventually find her wandering around on another floor entirely. The only time I can recall spending longer searching for a family member was when I mislaid two of my daughters in Ikea's marketplace and eventually located them in the food section salivating over the Swedish meatballs.

Spin me around once or twice on a featureless landscape and I'll happily retrace my outward route for miles without even noticing. All this is a roundabout way of saying that, having believed we were heading deep into the foothills of the Serra do Caldeirão, I was somewhat confused to find the waymarked café sitting there on the side of a main road. Had we somehow strayed off route? It appeared not. Two hours of hard uphill slog on a stony track had delivered us to the exact same location we could have reached if we'd jumped in a car in Loulé three minutes ago and put our foot down.

It's at times like these, that I wonder whether there's any real point in it? Hiking, I mean. Why do walkers spend eight or more hours trundling along, risking sunburn and blisters, dehydration and insect bites when lazier mortals reach the same destination in minutes? They marvel at the same landmarks, drink in the same bars and sleep in the same hotels, all with minimal effort. True, the off-road scenery can often be more spectacular and some of the places we've seen are inaccessible except by foot, but the protracted travelling time can feel so futile at times ... like now.

The roadside location of the café wasn't our only disappointment. Harri returned from the bar holding two of those teeny-weeny little bottles of lager which really shouldn't be served to anyone over fifteen! 'It *is* still only 11.30am,' Harri reprimanded me when he saw my crestfallen face. 'At this hour, the Portuguese would be drinking coffee.'

Despite the minuscule size of our drinks, it was pleasant enough sitting there in the covered seating area. There was only one other customer, a lady of around seventy who turned out to be from Liverpool. When we were leaving the route to come to the café, we'd passed a rather nice villa. It transpired the impressive property was her daughter's home and it was most probably going up for sale very soon. Our companion was just visiting and was amusing herself for a few hours while her digital nomad daughter worked from her home office.

We were keen to learn why anyone would want to leave such a gorgeous home in an idyllic location close to a decent-sized city and midway between the coast and the Serra do Caldeirão. It was the same story we'd heard before: the couple loved their adoptive country; however, there were no prospects here for their teenage children. It's disheartening to realise even people who achieve their dreams can be forced to abandon them due to circumstances beyond their control, in this case the economic slowdown and lack of opportunities for young people in inland Algarve.

We'd barely got going again when we encountered another familiar problem which had nothing to do with the economic climate – a group of over-excitable, untethered dogs. I'm not generally scared of dogs and it's many years since I had anything like a bad experience with them – most canines are more inclined to want to be my friend than to bite chunks out of me – but unfortunately, this lot seemed more vociferous and 'enthusiastic' than usual. Even when you like dogs, it can be disconcerting to have four of them hurtling towards you, barking like crazy. Our hiking shorts would have provided little protection had they chosen that moment to sink their teeth in our legs (or bottoms). So I did what I always do: I stood perfectly still and slowly extended my hand so that they could each have a good, long sniff of me before deciding if it was worth taking a bite of my flesh.

My gamble paid off. The larger two dogs took an instant liking to me, leaping to and fro as they vied for my attention, gently nipping the tips of my fingers as they rubbed their faces (and teeth) against my outstretched hand. Following their lead, the smaller dogs fell into step with us, all four having nothing better to do than trot happily along with us for the next few hundred metres, and then abruptly abandoning us to wander back from whence they'd come.

It was clearly going to be one of *those* days. First half measures of beer, then a potential dog attack and now sabotage of the worst kind. We couldn't believe our eyes when we encountered the first vandalised waymark. The wooden post was still there in the ground, but the attached Via Algarviana waymark panel had been prised off. We walked to the other side of the post to discover that waymark too had been removed.

When we walked the entire 300-kilometre trail, passing through various sized towns and villages along the route, we'd witnessed no vandalism whatsoever and had (perhaps naively) imagined local people were pleased, or at least accepting, of this new hiking initiative. We were clearly mistaken. In this rural location, it seemed someone was intent on thwarting the best intentions of the trail's founders.

As we continued walking, we realised waymark after waymark was missing. The wooden posts were there, but the familiar red and white stripes were gone. It looked as if the saboteur was following the trail and systematically destroying each one, presumably because they didn't want hikers walking on their land or near their property?

The thought that someone would deliberately sabotage the Via Algarviana saddened us. Apart from the ubiquitous graffiti – much of which is very artistic and/or political and often pleasing to both eye and intellect – we have seen very little evidence of vandalism in Portugal. This is not to say it doesn't happen, just that we have rarely seen it in rural Algarve. We wondered what had so infuriated the culprit that they were hell-bent on wrecking some innocuous waymarks. After all, the rationale behind the creation of this long-distance route was not only to attract serious hikers to areas ignored by most holidaymakers, but to bring much-needed tourist money to Algarve's inland villages and towns.

There was also a very serious side to these nasty-minded actions. The waymarks are there to supplement the maps produced by Almargem, to guide hikers through the rolling hills and ensure they do not go astray; many are positioned at track junctions or in locations where it may not be immediately obvious which path to follow. Some waymarks are not actually pointing you in any direction, but are prominently displayed red and white crosses to alert hikers to the fact that the way ahead is the wrong one and should not be followed. Having so many waymarks removed in a rural location where tracks frequently criss-cross one another was a recipe for disaster ... and likely to lead to many lost walkers.

Deliberately confusing people so that they inadvertently end up walking many kilometres in the wrong direction can have serious consequences in the high temperatures of an Algarve summer when there is a very real possibility of hikers running out of water. We like to think of ourselves as prepared when we set off for a long hike; however, even we underestimated the amount of water we'd need when we walked the section of the Via Algarviana between São Bartolomeu de Messines and Silves in May 2015. It's not an experience I care to repeat. There's nothing more terrifying to see your water levels diminishing rapidly when you still have a lot of tough walking ahead of you.

So what to do about the sudden lack of waymarking? Fortunately, Harri's academic training has turned him into something of an expert when a logical approach to problem solving is required. He deduced that any post which had been erected simply to stop people going that way would only have had a waymark on that one side (because no hiker would have approached it from the other direction). Waymarks which actually signified which way the link route went would have waymarks on both sides. By checking the back of each post for evidence of a waymark he was able to work out which posts were the 'right' ones and which had simply been put up to stop people going the wrong way. And so we proceeded slowly, checking the back of every post we encountered carefully to ensure we were going the right way.

We passed the highest point on the ridge, marked by an old stone windmill sporting a white trig point on its roof and began our long, slow descent over uneven, rocky terrain that rendered the downhill just as tough as the climbing had been.

This was the first backpacking trip where I didn't feel weighed down by my rucksack. The absence of a sleeping bag and foam mat (and for Harri, the tent and poles too) meant we had plenty of space. I was proud for resisting the temptation to fill it with too many non-essentials, reasoning that every additional pound I carried detracted exponentially from the enjoyment of the walking experience.

Our first-ever backpacking trip – five days walking the England Coast Path between Chepstow and Minehead (though we only made it to Watchet before we had to make a dash for our pre-booked train back to Wales) – had been far tougher than necessary simply because we'd been carrying so much weight. You soon realise what you can live without when you're long-distance hiking ... and, believe it or not, there are shops on route in most places (except mid-Wales ... only joking!).

This time around, I was enjoying the wonderful feeling of freedom that a lighter rucksack brings. I could put up with having to wear the same (washed but un-ironed) silk top every day, if it meant cantering up hills and galloping down the other side. Even so, I had managed to squeeze in a waterproof, long trousers and a change of footwear. Just in case, of course.

Having successfully circumnavigated the stretch without waymarks, we now joined the Fonte Benémola hiking trail. After hours without seeing a soul, there were suddenly people everywhere. Harri's ten-minute car park rule never fails. In this instance, the car park was located at nearby Fica Bem. No-one seemed to be carrying rucksacks so we guessed they were all following the 5km circular route.

It's a beautiful valley and it's easy to see why it's so popular with people who just want to stroll amidst beautiful surroundings. The Fonte Menalva is fed by local springs – the Olho and the Fonte Benémola – and, thanks to a series of weirs built along its course, it is one of the few streams in Algarve's *barrocal* region which retains significant water levels during the summer months (60%). As a result, the vegetation is more verdant than would otherwise be the case, providing varied habitats for birdlife. We ventured down to the waters' edge where walkers not continuing to Salir can easily cross the stream on raised concrete stepping stones, before settling down at a nearby bench to have a bite to eat.

Historically, this area's springs were found to have medicinal qualities – pray, find me a spring which did not! In 1928, Professor Charles Lepierre analysed the water in the Olho and found it to contain calcium bicarbonate and magnesium sulphate and be low in salt. People came from far afield to bathe in the stream, hoping its medicinal properties would improve rheumatic and skin problems.

Before you come rushing up from Quarteira or Vilamoura to leap into this pretty stream, you should perhaps know that the Olho's present-day waters are the very opposite of health-promoting. In 2012, tests revealed that the stream was contaminated by bacteria and micro-organisms, and the water unfit for human consumption.

After centuries of farming and cultivation in the valley, its farms and terraces were finally abandoned in the 1970s/1980s, presumably because agricultural on a small-scale had become uneconomic. In the succeeding decades, the land has been reclaimed by nature – and what a marvellous job it's done. An interpretation board assured me that the landscape I gazed upon was populated by ash trees, ash trees, poplars, tamarisks, silver willows, palms, snowball bushes, sugar canes, reeds, blackberry bushes, orchids and oleander. And hidden in their midst were kingfishers, tits, bee-eaters, herons, blackbirds, nightingales, blackcaps, grouses and bats. If we balanced on the water's edge in silence, we might perhaps spy a turtle, newt or toad, perhaps even an otter. We scanned the shallow water enthusiastically, but alas saw nothing.

A year or so after we moved into our Welsh village home, the conifer forests on one of the nearby slopes were felled. To the inexpert eye, the hillside appeared devastated, plundered. Harri shrugged his shoulders – these things happen – however, I was dismayed. The path through the woods – so familiar to us – formed part of the 27-mile Sirhowy Valley Walk from Newport to Tredegar. Now, the towering conifers and shadowy trails had gone, leaving an ugly tract of deeply rutted land in their wake. Where the ground was once cushioned with pine needles, we were now forced to snake our way through mountains of mud and deep, flooded trenches. For months, I was heartbroken at the destruction of our mountain and kept away.

There was one good point: the extensive local tree felling meant we could suddenly and unexpectedly gaze at our highest local mountain Twm Barlwm, see the ridge beyond. Our feet might be sinking in mud but now we could look across the valley and marvel at the lines of houses that meandered across the landscape or gaze over their chimney pots to admire the green slopes of nearby hills.

Within a year or two, we realised we no longer mourned the loss of the light-blocking larch trees. Young saplings were sprouting on the hillside. These weren't evergreen species, rather indigenous broadleaf trees, like beech and oak. In an astonishingly short time, nature had restored the landscape – and ecosystem – to its wild aka natural state.

Gazing across the beautiful Fonte da Benémola valley four decades after it had been abandoned by limestone quarrying and farming was again testament to nature's restorative powers.

The only one word to describe the climb out of the valley was arduous. Some of these limestone cliffs soar to heights of one hundred metres. While it was nothing like as hot as when we'd walked the Via Algarviana, it was too warm to be clambering up a steep trail that didn't seem likely to level off anytime soon. The rock underfoot was loose and slippery, a reminder that I was only one misplaced foot away from a painful stumble.

On and on we plodded, until we rounded a bend and came face to face with a couple heading in the opposite direction. The first thing I noticed was the woman – who looked to be around sixty – was wearing only shorts and a flesh-coloured bra. She didn't seem the slightest bit embarrassed to encounter us in her indecorous state and smilingly assured us that we had almost reached the top.

Clothed or not, she was right and it wasn't long before the trail levelled off and we could at last see Salir in the distance. The hilltop village was still a long way off with plenty of ups and downs inbetween here and our next beer; however, it was reassuring to know it was now on the horizon (for a short time anyway) because our legs were already starting to protest at their prolonged and unaccustomed use.

The inclement British weather aside, the problem had been working too hard. For the first summer in years, both Harri and I had abandoned too many weekends of hiking for long days at home hunched up over our computers.

Jobs must be like buses, because no sooner had I started working part-time at a Newport charity than a former contact offered me freelance work. I'd spent the winter months working hard, but didn't anticipate being stuck inside all summer too. Harri was equally busy with his own freelance work. Running keeps us fit, but it's the long-distance walking that really builds our stamina – and we hadn't done any serious hiking for months. Two days into this hiking holiday and we were already struggling.

Salir's most prominent landmark – its water tower – had disappeared from view and for a while, as we headed steeply downhill into the valley, it felt like we were heading in completely the wrong direction. Knowing we'd be clambering up said hill again in the morning as we retraced our steps back to Loulé didn't exactly help.

Our last few kilometres were through agricultural land and we picked our way through red-clay fields, along stone-walled paths and past small farms. I stopped occasionally to pluck an overripe pomegranate from a tree and could have gathered carob pods by the hundred had I been able to think of an immediate use for them.

I wasn't altogether sure what carob was used for, except I remembered it being a key ingredient in some of the expensive 'health' bars I used to buy (in my childfree days). One blogger brilliantly describes carob (*alfarroba*) as the 'love child' of chocolate and fig, going on to explain that Portugal is one of the top producers of carob worldwide. It seemed a shame that so much of it was going to waste here on the outskirts of Salir, but there wasn't much point in gathering it up ourselves.

Salir sits atop a hill which rises steeply from the valley floor. The town grew up around a Moorish castle during the Almohad period (12th and 13th centuries) before being taken over by invading Portuguese forces under Paio Peres Correira (d.1275). One theory regarding the town's name is that it derives from the Arabic word for 'escape', called out by the town's Muslim defenders as they fled in panic. I couldn't imagine ever wanting to escape this enchanting place.

We first visited Salir while walking the Via Algarviana (the 16km section from Barranco do Velho finished here). Then, the town had seemed like a metropolis, coming as it did after overnight stops at Balurcos, Furnazinhas, Vaqueiros and Cachopo. This time, we'd come straight from Loulé, with the result that Salir felt small and traditional, unspoilt and enchanting.

There's something rather special about returning to a place you've visited and adored previously. We headed up to the square where this time it was possible to enter the ground floor of the water tower and indulge in panoramic views of the Serra do Caldeirão. I won't rant about trees again, but let's just say that some of the best views of the nearby hills were somewhat obscured by unrestrained growth of vegetation alongside the water tower.

One of the best things about walking this link route to Salir was being able to spend a second night at the magical Casa da Mãe (take a minute to listen to the website – yes, that's right, *listen* to it).

A word of warning here ... if you're accustomed to staying at four- or five-star hotels where everything runs like clockwork, then Casa da Mãe (the name means 'mother's house') perhaps isn't for you. Oh, and it's probably helpful if you're a dog lover.

The original house at Casa da Mãe dates back to the 1920s, and the current owners began to renovate the property in 1995, transforming outbuildings and the hayloft into high-quality tourist accommodation. Throughout the gardens, there are tiled walkways and terraces adorned with flowerbeds and potted plants, lots of decorated benches and a good-size swimming pool.

On our last visit, we stayed in the twin-bedded Quarto Azul (the Blue Room), a converted outbuilding where almonds and carob were once stored, but on this occasion we were allocated the much larger Quarto Rosa (Pink Room), which had an adjoining living room and dining room (the interlinking door was unlocked but, as we were only staying for one night, we didn't make use of these additional facilities).

Having assigned us to a room, it seemed once again the key to the door had gone missing. Fortunately, on this occasion the door had been left open so we could at least get inside ... although ideally we'd have liked to be able to lock it when we ventured out later to eat.

Graciete was determined to find the missing key, so while Harri headed into our room to get ready for a swim, I dutifully trotted back to reception with her and her dog. She's a lovely woman who exudes warmth and speaks fluent French but unfortunately no English, meaning our conversation was restricted to say the least.

I waited in the reception area which seems to double as the couple's living room while Graciete and her husband hunted far and wide for the missing key: on the key rack, in various drawers, in brightly-coloured pots. As they pulled the place apart, they were completely oblivious to their pooch's antics. Said animal – a cross between a pug and a gremlin – had clearly forgotten how he was supposed to behave towards paying guests and was busily giving my right leg a vigorous licking from ankle to knee.

I hopped from one leg to the other, trying to detach him without causing a scene or deterring his good-natured owners from their search, but it was no good. My legs were sweaty and dirty ... exactly what he liked.

Every few minutes, Graciete would look up and fire questions at me in Portuguese, French and German, presumably updating me on their search results. I nodded and shook my head as seemed appropriate, and then she was off again. Meanwhile the pooch had remembered that humans generally have two legs and had started work on my left leg.

After much searching, the key to our room was eventually found and I returned to find Harri already in the pool. If I was a swimmer I might have joined him, but by now it was well after 5pm and too late in the autumn afternoon to venture into the unheated water. Instead, I decided upon a warm shower – my legs might be sparkling clean but the rest of me needed a wash.

It was dark but still warm when we headed back into Salir. Stars twinkled in the clear night sky and, despite it being early October, the evening had a sultry feel. Papagaio Dourado was busier than it had been in May but the owner was just as friendly and immediately led us to a table. Harri stuck to his favourite *espetadas* (huge juicy chunks of beef on skewers) and I opted for the sea bass. Sadly, both meals were served with chips and there was football on the telly – some things, it seems, never change. Not even in Salir.

As Harri noted, 'It is a truth, universally acknowledged, that on every television in every bar in Portugal there will always be a game of football being played'.

For photographs visit uk.pinterest.com/thewalkerswife

DAY 2: SALIR TO LOULÉ

We were pretty certain we'd managed to renegotiate breakfast from the usual nine o'clock to half an hour earlier. 'Pretty certain' rather than absolutely certain because I'd made our arrangements in long-forgotten schoolgirl French and Graciete, being the warm, gracious host she is, had nodded cheerfully throughout my mumblings but not actually repeated the new time. Had she actually understood anything I'd uttered, or was it simply good manners that prompted the smiles and nods?

It transpired that I had been understood, for when we presented ourselves in the breakfast room just after eight-thirty a table for two had been laid and someone was bustling around in the kitchen.

Once again, the breakfast was delicious and there was far more on our table that we really needed. The local goat's cheese (*queijo de cabra fresco*) has a much more delicate flavour than the goat's cheese I buy at home and a consistency more like cottage cheese. I trickled local honey over my umpteenth slice like João in Furnazinhas had shown me to do, wondering how I'd ever questioned the combination of flavours would be anything but delicious. The bread rolls had been warmed for us and – as Casa de Mãe didn't appear to have any other overnight guests – those we didn't eat would likely go to waste. We couldn't have that, so stuffed them with leftover ham and cheese to take with us.

While we were browsing through some publications in the breakfast room, we'd spotted the visitor book with a photograph of two mountain bikers visiting Casa de Mãe slipped inside the cover. We were tickled pink when, just as we were leaving, Graciete came rushing out to ask if we'd be willing to pose for a photograph outside the establishment? Once she'd done the honours, I took a photograph of her with Harri and the leg-licking hound. Who knows? Maybe we'll be cover stars on a future visitor book?

The mountain air felt a little bit nippy this morning so I ignored Harri's advice to the contrary and set off in my fleece. We were barely ten minutes out of town when I realised I was already far too hot in my outfit and would be at serious risk of overheating when we started climbing. Harri stood at the roadside watching me strip my top layer off with that smug look on his face that said 'I told you so'. He loves being proved right!

The thing is I'm so terrified of being cold that I often wear too many clothes. On a backpacking holiday, it isn't such a big issue because I'd be carrying the extra clothing whether it's on my back or in a rucksack. On day hikes, however, it's frustrating to have an extra-heavy pack to lug around simply because I over-estimated the amount of layers I'd need.

It was good to be walking in warm sunshine in October and though we were simply retracing our steps at this stage, the landscape looked very different in the clear, morning light. On the outskirts of Salir, a Portuguese foreman appeared to be giving one of his road workers unwarranted grief. Crikey, I thought, I wouldn't like to work here if it's okay to abuse your employees so vocally in a public place.

As we got closer, we could see what the problem was – there was a truck at the roadside and one of its wheels was covered with tarmac. We guessed the worker in question had been sloppy in his aim, with the result that there was now a sticky (and costly in terms of time) mishap to sort out. The foreman's fury was understandable. We walked past, doing our best not to look too interested in the contretemps while making certain we kept our feet well clear of the spillage.

One of Harri's countless theories is that a hiker never recalls the downhill sections of a route, but recalls in painful detail every step of a steep incline. As yesterday's walking had seemed mostly uphill (apart from the level stretch alongside the stream), we were looking forward to mostly walking downhill as we made our way back to Loulé.

In 2008, Fonte da Benémola was recognised as a place of great natural beauty and awarded the status of Local Protected Landscape, I guess putting it on the same footing as an Area of Outstanding Natural Beauty in the UK. It meant the place was popular with locals as well as overseas visitors like us, but it was enjoyable to be able to nod our heads and murmur *'bom dia'* or *'boa tarde'* instead of having only each other – and untethered dogs – for company.

Like people, Harri and I are mostly deskbound when we're not on holiday, which means it takes a while for our legs to receive the right 'long-distance hike' signals from our brains and to get into our stride.

The first few days are always a struggle. We have to ease ourselves into walking the way manual cars used to work up the gears: first gear (day one) barely gets us away from the kerb and moving, while second gear (day two) is really about easing ourselves into the flow of traffic. On day three (third gear) we start ramping up the speed a bit, although progress can still be hindered with too many stops and starts. It's not until day four when we really start accelerating and the journey becomes smooth and enjoyable.

Clearly we were acclimatising to the unaccustomed walking faster than usual. Yesterday – day two – we were unable to summon up sufficient energy to follow the 550-metre *uphill* detour to the pretty hilltop village of Querença, but in third gear we found ourselves positively charging up the steep road to this picturesque place with its quintessential *praça*. It's one of the things I adore most about Portuguese culture ... the notion that hanging out in the *praça* is a perfectly acceptable way of whiling away your day. You never see people rushing in the *praça*, indeed not. Instead, it's all very leisurely and civilised, sitting around with friends, sipping those tiny coffees and enjoying just *being*.

The *praça* provides ample outdoor space to host the weekly market and occasional festival. It's reminiscent of Britain's village green, though without the overgrown grass, puddles and mud. With *its* whitewashed church (Igreja da Nossa Senhora da Assunção), large stone cross, cafe bars and magnificent views across the Serra do Caldeirão, the *praça* here in Querença was one of the prettiest we've visited.

One of the most popular festivals in the village calendar is the chouriço festival held every January. This popular dish is made with pork shoulder, garlic, paprika, black pepper and red wine, and is likely to appear on the table at anytime during the day.

Pork is a mainstay of the Portuguese diet and Querença's festival offers thanks to São Luís, the patron saint of animals, for his care of the pigs in the vicinity. Clearly, this is a subjective viewpoint, and the pigs destined for the *chouriço* cooking pot could be justified for thinking their long-term well-being has been somewhat compromised!

The Portuguese love their festivals – a Christmas one here in Querença celebrates the humble cabbage – and all the eating and drinking that accompanies them, while visitors don't need an excuse to join in the merriment. Who were we to question the logic of celebrating the lives of pigs destined for the cooking pot when annual festivities like this one injected some much-needed life into Algarve's depopulated communities?

Intrigued by the signage, we popped into the Pólo Museológico da Água, a small museum about water. The interpretation panels were in Portuguese only and so, after a perfunctory look around, more of out of politeness than anything, we thanked the custodian and headed outside. The sun was hot in the sky, meaning it was definitely beer o'clock. We joined the other people-watchers outside a cafe, where Harri impressed the German family sitting on the neighbouring table by helping them to order their drinks. He's pretty good at languages, just don't tell him I said so.

It had been difficult to know what to pack for our autumn trip. My lightweight wardrobe had to cover every eventuality, from an Indian summer to blustery downpours and chilly breezes. The fabric type needed careful consideration too, as clothing worn next to our bodies would need to be washed and dried overnight (or at least pegged to our rucksacks).

A long-distance hike isn't the time to experiment with new clothes, or pack items that are usually too tight in the hope they might fit/flatter after a few days on the road ... believe me, unless you're walking in the wilderness where food is hard to come by, you'll be disappointed.

Southern Algarve is known for its warm temperatures and year-round sunshine, but this trip would see us heading into the mountains again, as well as walking on the wetter, windier Atlantic coast. In May, shorts and silk tops had served me well, but would they be sufficient in October?

After much head-scratching and debating, packing and repacking, I eventually decided upon these items: two pairs of shorts, one pair of long trousers, two vest tops (after the sad demise of my favourite silk camosole while walking the Via Algarviana I'd managed to find a similar one – also silk – in a charity shop), one smart but crease-free long-sleeved top for possible nights out, a stretchy long-sleeved underlayer, a short-sleeved top for warmer nights out and two fleeces – one medium thickness and one thinner. For some inexplicable reason, I also threw in the most unflattering bright yellow, high-necked, airtex teeshirt, my 'reward' for finishing the Gloucester 20 race.

It was this fashion *faux-pas* that I'd chosen to wear today – and was now regretting. My swinging camera case went some way towards hiding the teeshirt's clinginess, but I couldn't have felt more conspicuous (and ridiculous) as I sat outside the bar in Querença. I looked like a giant, shiny grapefruit amidst tables of sophisticated European tourists.

As is often the case on a sunny afternoon, one beer turned into two, and we began to wax lyrically about our surroundings. Querença, with its cobbled streets, decorative chimneys and extensive mountain views, was as pretty as a picture, we agreed, and well worth the detour and climb. The provision of clean, modern public toilets (and the impressively tiled ladies/men signs) in this little community certainly put the facilities in our home city of Newport (the remaining few which have survived 'austerity' cuts, that is) to shame.

The *praça* even had an open air stage, which made us wonder if Querença is the sort of place which attracts cultural and arty types. Enchanting as we found the village – and its beer – we were only halfway through our hike. Unless we wanted to be walking in the dark, it was time to get moving.

It felt more like a hot summer's day than mid-October as we headed back down the hill towards the medieval cobbled lane that would return us to our route. Harri and I have rarely retraced our steps, except when we were attempting to walk the Cambrian Way and then only from necessity and needing to return to our parked car each day. Then, Harri usually found some way of turning the day's walking into a circular route or at least change certain sections of it.

Now we found ourselves walking the exact same route as yesterday, albeit it in the opposite direction, and we were surprised to discover that it wasn't anywhere near as tedious as we imagined. For a start, all yesterday's tough climbs were now transformed into downhill sections. Instead of puffing and panting and focusing on nothing except reaching the top of the next hill, we were now able to gaze around and appreciate our surroundings.

Approaching the twists and turns of the track from a different direction, we noticed aspects of the landscape that had previously passed us by. As we strolled along narrow lanes and past traditional houses, it dawned on me that while you think you remember a route pretty clearly, you don't necessarily remember the landmarks in the right order. Relative distances, too, can become skewed in your mnd.

And so it was, we arrived at the café near Loulé much sooner than anticipated. We stopped, this time not for beer but intending to treat ourselves to icecreams. Alas, we'd forgotten that it was now October and, though hotter than the average summer day in Wales, Algarve's summer season was just about over. If it was icecream we wanted, we should have turned up a month earlier.

Walking the Via Algarviana had demonstrated that away from the tourist areas not everyone speaks English (indeed why should they?). I'd meant to learn a little more Portuguese vocabulary for this second trip. Unfortunately, whilst I set out with good intentions and was scoring full points for everything except my pronunciation (always my weak point, even in English), my initial enthusiasm had dwindled and I was now struggling to remember anything.

There'd been a minor confidence boost earlier today when we passed a sign saying Vale Mulher and I was able to translate 'valley of the woman', but on the whole I was feeling mighty ashamed of my linguistic apathy.

And it wasn't just language problems that were concerning me. On Sunday I'd run a very poor Cardiff Half Marathon; I'd struggled from mile 10 onwards and limped over the finish line. We flew to Faro the following day, giving me no opportunity to rest up and recuperate.

Yesterday, on route to Salir, my right foot decided it had had enough abuse for one week and a heel spur which had sprung up from nowhere had started hurting like crazy. I'd needed to pop four painkillers just to keep going and endured one of Harri's sadistic foot massages last night in the hope it might just help. It must have worked because my heel wasn't rubbing quite so much today; however, I was still concerned about aggravating it further by being on my feet all day.

Not one to be outdone on the ailments front, Harri was also claiming to be suffering from all manner of aches and pains. At various points in the day, he had complained about an aching shoulder, tight hamstrings and calf muscles and eventually declared a diagnosis of peroneal tendonitis.

We must have looked a strange sight, limping along with our real and imagined ailments, convinced all the exercise, running and long-distance hiking was keeping us fit and healthy, while giving every appearance of being a pair of rucksack-carrying wrecks.

It was approaching six o'clock when we strolled into Loulé, having enjoyed panoramic views to the coast for the latter part of the route. Thankfully the tourist information office was still open because, true to our word, we'd picked up a leaflet about Casa da Mãe. The same assistant was behind the counter and she seemed very pleased with this new information. Harri still finds it incredible that she hadn't heard of one of the only accommodation providers in a town just a quarter of an hour's drive away.

That fifteen-minute car journey had taken us all day to walk. We'd planned to return to the same restaurant tonight, but we were exhausted and couldn't face the thought of showering and going out again. There was a Continente supermarket on the main road into town; however, reaching it wasn't as straightforward as you'd think. I don't think it ever crosses the minds of those who design these vast superstores that someone might arrive on foot. Having tried – and failed – to identify a pedestrian route between the main road and the store's entrance, we had no choice but to walk along a vehicle-only ramp.

Can there be anything more exciting than perusing the shelves of a foreign supermarket? Maybe it's just me, but I could spend hours wandering around the aisles, tossing exotic fruits and vegetables, plus a whole load of delicious-looking foods, into my trolley. Well, perhaps not those vacuum-packed piglets or the whole octopuses, but it is hard not to be tempted by the unfamiliar sights and smells, especially the sugar-coated delights of the *padaria*.

Harri doesn't like supermarkets, foreign or otherwise, and he was getting fractious.

'The whole point of coming here was to quickly grab something to eat so we didn't have to go out again tonight,' he reminded me testily. 'It rather defeats the object if we spend the whole evening walking around a supermarket.'

It was time to focus on dinner. There wasn't a fridge in our room so we stuck to what we needed for tonight – a cooked chicken, olives, a whole mango – and some more goats' cheese for tomorrow. Last night in Salir we'd tried Somersby cider for the first time and had been surprised how much we enjoyed its strong apple taste. We tossed four bottles into our basket and headed to the checkout. That was dinner plus drinks sorted for under ten euros.

We headed back into town where we booked into the rather splendid Loulé Jardim Hotel for the second time in three days.

On Monday night, our double room had been spacious and beautifully decorated. In fact, we would have been perfectly happy to find ourselves in the same room and were actually a little disappointed to be directed to the top floor of the hotel ... until we opened our room door and stepped inside.

What a difference those two extra floors made in relation to the views. Our room had not one but two sets of French doors leading onto a terrace that wrapped around our spacious room. From up here, we had panoramic views across Loulé, the nearby mountains *and* the distant coastline. We were surprised to discover how many of the old properties had wonderful rooftop terraces as none were detectable from street level.

Had we been here in the summer months, there's no doubt we would eaten outside, but there was already an autumnal nip in the air so we settled for admiring the dazzling colours of the sun setting over the distant dome of Nossa Senhora da Piedade before heading inside for food.

For photographs visit uk.pinterest.com/thewalkerswife

DAY 3: HEADING TO PORTIMÃO

Our Algarve baptism of fire had involved three days of relatively tough walking so Harri thought it might be sensible to take things easier today. Believe me, I didn't need any persuading. While I fervently believe you *are* never too old to backpack, there is such a thing as overdoing it. After four days of hard physical activity, every inch of my body – and my poorly heel in particular – was craving a rest.

This morning we'd be retracing our steps to Loulé's out-of-town railway station; however, that was the only walking we actually *needed* to do. When we arrived in Portimão we intended to go out exploring and would probably cover several miles, but unusually there was no plan, no pre-planned route, and no pressure to get the distance done. The only absolute in today's itinerary was reaching Loulé station in time to catch our 10.40am train.

With memories of the uphill slog here two days ago, I realised with glee that our return walk would be mostly downhill and thus, much easier. It meant we had plenty of time to enjoy what must be one of the most lavish of breakfasts we've enjoyed in Algarve. In the dining room, we welcomed Monika like an old friend and enjoyed hearing what she'd been up to since we last talked. Like us, she's already fallen for Portugal big time and is planning to return next summer. I have nothing but admiration for people like her who are prepared to travel alone because it's preferable to the alternative, i.e. not travelling at all, or choosing the wrong travelling companion. Monika explained that she liked to linger, contemplate a scene or location, take photographs; this, she admitted, was difficult when your friends had different expectations of a holiday.

Her courage in coming to Portugal alone definitely seemed to have paid off – on her first two days of wandering she'd met plenty of kindred spirits and, while the time with her new friends was brief, each person will have contributed to the other's memories, as Monika has to ours. I particularly liked her huge appetite – watching this young Polish woman tucking into a large cooked breakfast certainly made me feel less greedy about my return trips to the buffet table.

Yes, we had a lovely leisurely breakfast. And then we missed our train.

Of course, there was a post mortem, conducted in the cafe opposite Loulé railway station during our two-hour wait for the next train. Here, Harri pinpointed my second dish of mango halves and pomegranate seeds as the deciding factor in our lax timekeeping. In his view, this was a mistake of epic proportions: *my* mistake.

We had cut things too fine, recalling too late how undulating the walk from the station actually was, remembering how it had in fact taken us longer than the hour-and-a-half we had allowed this morning.

Realising this, we had tried hard to make up the lost time. We scuttled along low-walled tracks, and past high-walled orange groves, vineyards, endless barking dogs, luxurious villas and dilapidated ruins. We jumped over a small stream and carried on past more barking dogs tethered to a kennel outside a rural building.

Around the half way point, it became obvious that we weren't going to catch this train unless we speeded up considerably. Eventually, we were power walking all but the very steepest uphill climbs and becoming very hot and sweaty in the process.

Despite it being October, there were fruit and vegetables growing everywhere, making us wonder if there is a second harvest in Algarve. Burst pomegranates clung to branches, others blanketed the ground below. We passed a field where marrow, butternut squash and pumpkins of enviable size lay abandoned on the rust-coloured soil. Veggie-envy was creeping in. At home in Wales, I'd lovingly tended my four by ten foot vegetable garden year after year, but was so far from being self-sufficient it was laughable.

One bumper year I'd managed to grow nine decent-sized squash, beating my green-fingered mother-in-law into the bargain, but it turned out to be a one-off. Over the past few summers, I'd enjoyed pitifully slim pickings. My latest crop had comprised a handful of strawberries, marginally more raspberries and three miniscule pumpkins. Most of the ground-level strawberries had been gobbled up by slugs and the courgettes were a no-show.

How I envied Portuguese gardeners who benefited from an abundance of sunshine and had far fewer slugs to deal with. And just to give you some idea of the injustice of it all, I've seen butternut squash sold *by the slice* here in Algarve, hinting at the magnitude of the whole vegetables.

I was happily daydreaming about living the 'good life', when Harri's voice cut through my thoughts.

'We're going to miss the train if you don't get a move on,' he reminded me for the umpteenth time.

'I know, I know,' I said, speeding up, while imagining a brown-armed, plaited version of myself lovingly tending rows of perfectly formed strawberry plants. Perhaps we could plant a small vineyard, surrounded by orange, lemon, mango and pomegranate trees. I'd always fancied pressing my own olive oil.

We reached Loulé station with thirty seconds to spare, and then made the fatal mistake of dithering for a split second while we worked out whether we needed to cross the footbridge to the platform opposite. We didn't notice our train in the station *waiting*. By the time we did, its automatic doors were already sliding shut. We ran towards the train, waving our arms desperately to indicate we were supposed to be on the train not standing on the platform. The train driver saw our dismayed expressions, but shook his head firmly: automatic doors are automatic doors. There was nothing he or we could do.

It was now I discovered the 10.40am to Portimão was in fact the 10.39am to Portimão. In my defence, there was a certain amount of confusion surrounding the actual distance we had to walk. The waymarked route was 7.5km and I'm confident we could have covered that in the hour and twenty minutes available to us. My undoing was not considering the extra kilometres of convoluted route around Loulé before we joined the link route.

I'd also forgotten the demanding nature of the route to the station. The only steep bit I recalled from the walk *to* Loulé was a difficult scrubby bank underneath the dual carriageway and yet, as we now discovered, there were several hills to slow us down.

Thirty seconds, that's all it takes. If I'd eaten one fewer mouthful of pomegranate, packed my rucksack slightly more quickly, hadn't faltered on the bank of the small stream which flowed across our route ... you see how Harri successfully convinced me that missing our train was my fault entirely. No mention of his own little delays, including that less than direct route out of Loulé.

We watched our train chug out of the station, then pondered on how to while away the two hours before the next one. There was precious little to do here on the far reaches of Loulé. Determined to find the positive in our predicament (and to stop Harri going on at me), I pointed out that if we had caught the 10.39am train as planned, we'd have been stuck with our rucksacks for several hours in Portimão. Missing the train meant our arrival would now coincide perfectly with the hotel check-in time. As our accommodation was located close to the station in readiness for an early departure tomorrow, it now made perfect sense to go straight there, offload everything and go exploring without the burden of rucksacks. Gradually, Harri started to see the logic in what I was saying and (I think) I was finally forgiven for succumbing to carnal sin in the form of mango and pomegranate seeds.

There was a small bar opposite the railway station with a shaded outside area. Given the circumstances, we decided we deserved an early beer while Harri caught up with yesterday's notes. In fact, as we settled down with our drinks, missing our train now seemed a rather genius idea.

I might have known Harri wouldn't let the subject of *my* tardiness drop for long. After a few minutes of writing, he looked up to remind me that I'd complained to Monika earlier how we always arrived everywhere – airports, bus stops, *train* stations – far too early due to his obsessive timekeeping. I suspect I'm never going to hear the end of this. Two hours later, a second train pulled into Loulé station and this time we made certain we were on it.

The railways arrived rather later in Portugal than in the UK. In the 1840s, the Victorians were growing accustomed to railway travel, but the first railway in Portugal was not inaugurated until 1856. The initial stretch of railway stretched from Lisbon to Carregado, to the north-east of the city. The present-day Linha do Algarve was created when two existing lines – Ramal de Lagos and the Linha do Sul were combined.

Unsurprisingly given their recently developed expertise, British engineers were involved in building some of Portugal's earliest railways. The National Railway Museum in York holds many papers written by English civil engineer Robert Johnson who helped develop several sections of railway in Portugal, including the Lagos to Vila Real section.

Johnson's surviving 1861 papers include estimated costs for the first section of the railroad between Tavira and Ponte de Cacella, distance calculations for the fifth section of the railroad from Tavira to Vila Real, calculations for embankments and earthworks and a map showing the proposed route from Lagos to Vila Real.

A rail journey through Algarve by rail is a wonderful experience as long as you're in no hurry to reach your destination. Don't expect sea views – or any views at all if you choose a carriage where the windows are obscured by graffiti – because the tracks, which long pre-date tourism, run mostly several kilometres inland.

Instead enjoy a journey as unhurried and relaxing as those enjoyed by Portugal's early railway passengers. One of the reasons for the speed, or lack of, is that the railway is mostly single track with few passing places. The only place it connects to the rest of the Portuguese railway network is Tunes.

Indeed, Tunes would have remained a small rural village had it not been for the railway. The original plans for a station at Algoz were abandoned due to the problematic terrain (it was too hilly) and the location was moved several kilometres east to an agricultural area dominated by vineyards. The railway workers moved in and the first train passed through Tunes on the Lisbon-Faro line on February 21, 1889.

Along this line, very town has its name painted in large lettering on the station building – much better than the small and easy-to-miss low-level platform signage in the UK. While it's true that many of these beautiful old Victorian stations have seen better days, what most ruins their appearance is the spray-paint graffiti that dominates the station building walls. This isn't street art of the kind you see in Lagos and other cities in Portugal, but just plain vandalism. In 2016, the authorities launched a clean-up programme; however, it remains to be seen if the mindless vandals will be deterred.

We wiled away a pleasant hour passing through the eight stations between Loulé and Portimão, including Albufeira (probably the best-known of all Algarve resorts), Tunes and Silves.

Our hotel was just minutes from Portimão station and we had no trouble finding it. Anything was going to be a letdown after the luxury of our Loulé hotel room with its breath-taking views and the Made Inn was exactly what we'd anticipated – the Portuguese equivalent of a

Travelodge. Our compact room was spotlessly clean with everything we needed, but there were no frills and no views. There would be no strolling out onto a private balcony to admire the sunset this evening; in fact, any strolling would have to be carefully choreographed if Harri and I were to avoid bumping into each other at the end of the bed.

That said, our aim was to be as close to the station as possible so that we could catch the 9am train to Mexilhoeira Grande, and this we had achieved. Our sloppy timekeeping had worked out well today but we had a lot of miles to cover tomorrow – an early start was imperative.

Unusually, we had nothing planned for the rest of the day. When Harri was typing up his notes earlier, he'd tossed me the Portimão map we'd bought for 50c on our last trip and told me to decide what I wanted to do. We planned to spend the rest of the afternoon exploring before finding somewhere to eat. When we returned to our overnight cubicle it would be only to shower and sleep.

With me in charge of exploration for a change, we headed through the city's lively cafe-filled streets and were pleasantly surprised to arrive at a wide promenade running along the west bank of the exquisitely turquoise Arade. We had no idea whether the promenade would take us all the way to the city's main beach of Praia da Rocha but it really didn't matter. For once, it was nice to be able to wander around without any definite plans ... or heavy rucksacks.

I was surprised to learn that Portimão is much larger than Lagos, although with populations of around 55k and 31k respectively; both cities are pint-sized compared to our home city of Newport (another port). Like Lagos, Portimão developed on the bank of a wide river, but while the Arade is considerably wider at the mouth than the canalised Bensafrim in Lagos the silting up of the busy channel is problematic.

In October 2016, the cruise ship Thomas Spirit ran aground with over 1,000 passengers on board while attempting to dock in the port of Portimão. Two months later, the Portuguese government announced the city would receive 20 million euros to dredge the channel and extend the quayside.

We passed the main port where an enormous German cruise ship was moored and continued towards the marina. Sitting on a low wall, we pondered the age-old question: is it better to live in a beautiful property looking out on an ugly view, or live in an ugly home with scenic surroundings. The question was particularly pertinent here on the Arade. Across the water, Ferragudo with its cluster of whitewashed houses was picture-postcard pretty, yet for those living in its gorgeous beachfront villas the landscape would be one of towering cranes, lines of shipping containers and unsightly, high-rise apartment blocks.

People living on the Portimão side of the estuary had yet more advantages in terms of scenic views: from here the medieval Forte de São João do Arade and its adjacent bay was clearly visible, while they would be hidden from sight for those living in the sheltered fishing village just a stone's throw away. And if the seventeenth-century fortification looks to be in pristine condition, it's because the property was once owned and used as a summer residence by the poet Coelho Carvalho.

The fort was built on the orders of King John IV, its position at the mouth of the Arade chosen for the purpose of defence (back in its heyday the fort boasted two batteries with seven pieces of artillery). Its soft-rock foundations meant it emerged unscathed from the Lisbon earthquake which caused so much destruction elsewhere in the Algarve region.

When its defensive role ceased, the fort was briefly used to monitor ships travelling up the Arade to Silves (the river is now only navigable for small pleasure boats). Eventually it fell into disuse, and was declassified as a fort in 1896. This imposing and beautiful property remains privately owned – which is a shame as I would have loved a look round – and, in 1976, was classified as a historic building by the Instituto Português do Património Arquitectónico (IPPAR).

Having baulked at the ridiculously high prices of the first restaurants we passed at Praia da Rocha (the beach is popular with international jet-setters), we decided to stop at O Faro at the top of the beach and enjoyed one of the nicest meals of the holiday for an incredibly good price (which I forgot to note). We chose one of the set meals – fish in orange sauce – with a bottle of rosé and sat outside to enjoy the late afternoon sunshine. Afterwards, we leaned back in our chairs and revelled in an unfamiliar languor while we watched a succession of runners passing by. The food, wine and ambiance were wonderful, demonstrating there is no need to part with a small fortune to enjoy fine cuisine at a seafront restaurant.

After our meal, we thought we should perhaps stretch our legs a bit more before returning to our hotel. Several of the runners had headed out to the lighthouse at the end of the pier (after which our restaurant was obviously named) so we strolled after them.

Praia da Rocha is an extraordinarily wide beach which has attracted tourists since the 19th century. Regrettably, modern and mostly unsightly developments now dwarf the 38-roomed Bela Vista Hotel, reputedly the first hotel in Algarve. The Bella Vista is a singularly stunning property and is right up there with the Hotel del Coronado in San Diego (where some of the scenes in the Marilyn Monroe film *Some Like It Hot* were filmed and a place I've been lucky enough to visit ... just for the one drink on the terrace, you understand).

In mid October, Algarve's main tourism season was obviously drawing to an end and there were few bronzed bodies filling the rows of sunbeds. Even the ubiquitous boat trip sellers had that jaded 'end of season' look about them and most barely raised an eyebrow as we sauntered past.

Turning to gaze upon modern-day Portimão from the end of the pier, we agreed our preferred view was the one from the restaurant.

It was time to leave the beach and head back to our hotel. We intended to take a detour to Lidl to stock up on supplies for tomorrow when we'd be walking from Mexilhoeira Grande to Monchique; it promised to be a long day with an early start so we wouldn't have time to go shopping in the morning.

This was where our street map came in handy and, using it in conjunction with online mapping, Harri expertly identified a footpath which weaved between the high-rise buildings and criss-crossed through an unexpected area of scrubland.

Back in the built-up area, we were surprised to hear birdsong, well more bird heavy metal simply because it was so loud. We looked up to see what appeared to be hundreds of small birds swooping in and out of the branches of a nearby tree, singing their little hearts out and, to all appearances, having a whale of a time. It was an uplifting sight, and more so because we were now in the middle of in the concrete jungle that is Portimão.

The turquoise waters and the gorgeous views across the Arade were starting to feel like a distant memory as we wandered through this highly populous area dominated by high-rise apartment blocks attempting to get back to our hotel. The ugliness of the built landscape aside, we were also having fun trying to cross the roads; the traffic in Portimão was heavier than anything we'd previously encountered in Algarve.

We were tired and had a long day ahead of us tomorrow. Officially today had been a non-walking day, but Harri did a quick calculation and reckoned we'd clocked up around 16km at the very least. Best of all, my heel had ceased to hurt.

For photographs visit uk.pinterest.com/thewalkerswife

DAY 4: MEXILHOEIRA GRANDE TO MONCHIQUE

There was a hurricane heading our way. And because it originated on the other side of the Atlantic, it had a name. It was Monika's mother who alerted her to this depressing news, and Monika shared the news with us.

Hurricane Joaquin first hit the Bahamas and east coast of America; however, now it was heading towards continental Europe, with the worst ravages of the extreme weather forecast for Algarve's west coast – exactly where we were headed tomorrow. Harri warned me to expect rain – and plenty of it – over the next few days. It seemed our 'precautionary' measure of bringing lightweight waterproofs and full-length trousers might not have been precautionary enough.

This was not what I wanted to hear. He might have been downgraded to a 'tropical storm' but Joaquin was still an unwelcome companion on my hiking holiday.

The more I thought about it, the more ridiculous the practice of naming hurricanes seemed. I mean it's not as if the name reflects any aspect of their personality. It was only later we learned that Joaquin was a killer, a mass-murderer who was responsible for the death of 34 merchant navy sailors aboard the ill-fated SS El Faro (the ship was from the US, despite its name). It simply feels wrong to personify something as random and merciless as a hurricane.

In Algarve, Joaquin's wrath had yet to arrive and the day started well enough if you ignore the bidet episode. Bidets are one of those things you either love or hate, like marmite and sprouts. I fall into the 'not a big fan' category; however, Harri thinks bidets are the pinnacle of human sophistication and never wastes an opportunity to use one (though not always for the purpose they were intended).

Yesterday, he'd had a bit of an accident while rising from a bidet. He'd tried to stand up quickly on stiff legs, stumbled forward and nearly hit his head on the sink. Being a bit of a drama queen (when I'm off duty), he'd reported seeing his whole life flashing before him as he flew through the air. As a result, he was a little bit apprehensive with today's bidet lest his luck ran out. I understood entirely. I mean, who wants their last seconds on earth to be a close encounter with a ceramic bottom-washing basin?

My own light bulb moment regarding the usefulness of the humble bidet was in France (from where the bidet is thought to originate) when my middle daughter, then around four, thought it a good idea to emulate her slightly inebriated mother who had decided it would be fun to run around our hotel's rather formal gardens like a ... well, like a slightly inebriated Brit. While I leapt joyously over the line of rose bushes, my daughter, having what she frequently reminded me were 'only little legs', didn't quite clear the first rose bush and landed bottom first on a bed of thorns. Back in our ornate but outdated hotel room, the presence of the never-before-seen bidet proved a godsend for a small and sore posterior.

Danger it seems lurks in the most unexpected of places. One of the funniest things I ever read, was a chapter in Bill Bryson's *Notes from a Big Country* where he recounted some home accident statistics from the *Statistical Abstract of the United States*. Bryson was confounded by the many everyday risks lurking in our everyday lives. Some are obvious – stairs, razors, chainsaws – with others less so: sofa beds, pencils, *ceilings*. Scouring the statistics, Bryson came to the reluctant conclusion that he was 'far more likely to be hurt by my ceiling or underpants ... than by a stranger'. He does not mention bidets in his article, perhaps because they are less popular in the US than in mainland Europe, but I feel someone should whisper a warning in his ear before his next visit.

Still on the subject of underpants, a former colleague of ours must take the biscuit for underwear-related injuries. Eager to improve his fitness, while acknowledging his early-morning reluctance to actually get out there pounding the streets, Ade decided to go to bed dressed in his running kit, socks and all. The only problem was he forgot he was wearing running socks when he was caught by the call of nature in the middle of the night, and leapt onto the laminated bedroom floor – the *slippery*, laminated bedroom floor – at the speed of light, skated across the room like Bambi with arms flailing and crashed full-on into the facing wall.

I'd love to have been a fly on the wall when he reported to A&E at two in the morning having nearly knocked himself out in his own bedroom.

Our hotel room might not have been memorable, but the breakfast wasn't half bad and, with the railway station just a few minutes' walk away, at least I didn't have to endure one of Harri's looks when I returned to the buffet table for seconds.

Given that Portimão to Mexilhoeira Grande is roughly half the distance of Newport to Cardiff we could be forgiven for expecting our 9.30am train to get there twice as fast, but no such luck. We couldn't grumble about the price though – just €1.40 each compared to well over £4 for a single from our local station to Cardiff Central.

Once again, the railway station was just outside the village, though nowhere near as distant as Loulé's, and naturally it was covered with spray paint and scrawled names. Our onward route into town was straightforward and reasonably level and we were soon standing in another tree-lined *praça* in front of another whitewashed church.

We'd been steadily climbing since we got off the train and the views of the surrounding countryside and salt marshes were charming. This was certainly the place to 'stand and stare' to steal Newport poet W H Davies' immortal words, though why anyone would ever need to stand in Mexilhoeira was a mystery. There were benches aplenty, certainly sufficient seating for a Roman army to stop here for lunch, but alas no public toilets.

Impressed with the general ambiance of the place, I added the village to my list of potential places to live, though Harri was quick to point out that I might have as much trouble with the pronunciation as I do with some of the place names in Wales. Portuguese pronunciation (a word which itself is frequently mispronounced) generally follows strict rules, but where the letter 'x' is concerned it's less clear cut: that impish letter can be pronounced in any of three ways and there are no rules to determine which one is right. Fortunately, there aren't very many Portuguese words with an 'x' in them.

Its difficult-to-pronounce name aside, Mexilhoeira Grande positively oozed charm, was located a stone's throw from the stunning Alvor lagoon and was within walking distance of a railway station on a line that could quickly transport you to Lagos in one direction and, albeit more slowly, deliver you to Albufeira, Faro and Tavira in the other. It's also a place with a long history.

Roman troops arrived on the Iberian peninsula for the first time in 219BC. For the next 200 years, they fought the local population and by 19BC, the Roman Republic controlled almost the entire peninsula and had incorporated most of what was later to become Portugal into the province of Lusitania. Their old enemies, the Carthaginians, were expelled from the province and their coastal colonies taken over. A focal point for Roman settlement was Lagos (*Lacobriga*) with its important harbour (Lacobriga), and several Roman ruins have been found in the area, including in the vicinity of Portimão (*Portus Magnus*).

Close to Mexilhoeira are the remains of the large Roman villa of Abicada, which was first excavated in 1917 and became a National Monument in 1940. Research has determined that the villa dates back to the first century AD. My favourite element of any Roman ruin (and in Wales we live close to the Roman towns of Caerleon and Caerwent), are the mosaic floors; however, thanks to the mindless vandalism of a few, the extensive mosaic floors at Abicada had to be removed from their original site a few years ago and transferred to Portimão museum for safe keeping. We didn't feel a floorless villa warranted a detour, especially as we had a long uphill hike today; however, the remaining walls do look quite impressive on Google Earth.

We had known from the outset that today's walking – link route 3 on the Via Algarviana – was going to be tough. The 25.4km distance didn't sound too bad, but the projectory was mostly uphill with 818 metres of accumulated climbing. The online guide helpfully noted that the route was 'difficult', though having walked to Monchique from Silves previously I think we'd worked that one out for ourselves.

The sun was as hot as yesterday, keeping me in denial about the imminent arrival of Joaquin. It just didn't seem possible that the weather was going to change so dramatically overnight. Maybe 'he' wasn't going to visit the Iberian coastline after all? Harri shook his head glumly. He takes his meteorology seriously: if the tail end of a hurricane was predicted, then mentally prepare for one we must.

We followed a succession of tracks and minor roads, passing through the pretty village of Figuiera, until eventually a familiar striped waymark directed us upwards and onto scrubland. Happy to be leaving the road's hard surface for a while, we trotted along in single file, climbing steadily for a time before the track levelled off and narrowed. Now we were walking parallel to the road and, glancing down, it occurred to me that the tarmac surface looked a long way down. Many sections of our levada walking on Madeira had been of a vertiginous nature and I experienced an unwelcome sense of *déjà vu*.

My alarm increased when we rounded a bend and the footpath we'd been following suddenly vanished. To my right was a crumbling cliff, to my left a sheer drop onto the road. Completely unnerved, I did what any sensible hiker would do: I froze. I could see Harri forging ahead, but as much as I willed them to keep moving, my feet were glued to the spot.

Overcome with panic, I made the rash – and ultimately unwise – decision to retrace my steps. As I turned, I was vaguely aware that Harri was calling me, but by now all the only thing on my mind was getting back to solid ground. My heart hammering, I tried to follow the footpath back to the scrubland, failed to notice a fork in the path and ended up shuffling along on a narrowing *higher-level* ledge.

'What on earth are you doing?' Harri's voice rang out from behind. 'Stay exactly where you are and don't move.'

I'd have struggled to do anything else. Having belatedly realised my predicament, I was now clinging terrified to the cliff face, tears spilling down my cheeks.

'Don't worry, I'm coming to get you,' he called.

Harri placed his rucksack on the ground and cautiously edged his way along the cliff path towards me.

'Hand me your rucksack and I'll come back for you,' he instructed, when he drew up close. I did what he asked, careful not to glance down as I wriggled out of my rucksack and ever-so-slowly held it out to him.

Within minutes, he had deposited it alongside his own and was back at my side. This time Harri held my hand and led me very slowly back along the ledge and to safely. Once we had reached the wider stretch of footpath where he'd left our rucksacks, Harri explained what we were going to do next.

It transpired that while I'd been imitating a mountain goat, Harri had been trying to work out if there was some way we could safely clamber down to the road. If we hadn't been carrying rucksacks, he thought we might have been able to sit down and jostle our bottoms down the steep decline. With rucksacks, however, our balance would be askew, making a tumble likely.

'Our only option is to follow the footpath back to the road,' Harri concluded. 'I know it's not ideal, but there's no point risking life and limb to save half an hour.'

I could have kissed him there and then, but having wasted so much time already, I thought it best just to follow.

Thirty minutes later, we were gazing up at the offending cliff from the road. From this vantage point, it was obvious there had been a recent landslide and that the onward section of footpath linking back to the road no longer existed. Hopefully, the waymarks will be redirected soon so that no-one else is put at risk.

We'd hoped to get a beer in the tiny hamlet of Poio; however, the only restaurant was not due to open until this evening so our plans were thwarted. At this point, I redeemed myself by remembering that I had stashed a can of beer in my rucksack (left over from last night) and we settled down at the edge of some agricultural fields to enjoy it.

After Poio, we stuck to the traffic-free road, enjoying the warm sunshine and peacefulness of our surroundings. We passed numerous *quintas* in sizeable grounds set back from the road, all of which looked abandoned or at least as though the owners had fallen on hard times. Many *quintas* with agricultural land were forcibly expropriated following the 1974 Portugal revolution in the name of land reform. In 1978, the democratically elected government began the process of returning the quintas to their legal owners, but not everyone returned to farm their original land.

I have no idea if the fate of the properties we were now passing were linked with Portugal's land reforms – maybe they were abandoned for altogether different reasons – but the gradual disappearance of what must once have been beautifully laid out and well-tended gardens saddened the latent horticulturalist in me.

The landscape changed again and we found ourselves walking through relatively flat, agricultural land with sweeping rust-soiled fields. Here, the properties were functional, their residents more concerned with working the land than installing pretty terraces and swimming pools.

At one point, the track became perilously steep with loose stones underfoot and I reached out to steady myself on plants growing alongside the path, realising too late that I'd just grabbed a handful of sticky cistus leaves.

Lunch was a messy affair. We'd been walking for hours and mostly climbing. It was 2.30pm and we were hot, hungry and thirsty. When it became obvious no scenic picnic spot was going to reveal itself anytime soon, we perched on two large rocks at the side of the road.

Thanks to Lidl in Portimão, I'd been able to make chicken and goat's cheese rolls this morning. They were delicious and straightforward to eat: I wish I could say the same about the large, heavy mango I'd purchased in Loulé and had been lugging around ever since. It was time to rid myself of the unnecessary weight; however, I hadn't bargained for its juiciness or the difficulty of cutting a large, ripe mango with the tiny knife on Harri's Victoriana Swisscard Lite. Well, I'd always assumed it was a knife but the company website describes it as an 'emergency blade' (letter opener) which might explain why I was reduced to chiselling rather than slicing through the dripping, over-ripe fruit. Thank goodness Harri never ventures far without a pack of wet wipes!

Sod's law was working well today, for we'd no sooner set off again when we came across a stream with a small waterfall and several large boulders at the water's edge. This perfect dipping spot was Harri's idea of paradise, but, alas, our lunch was eaten and we needed to press on if we were ever to reach Monchique.

The next few miles saw us trekking through a narrow valley with steep scrubby sides broken by frequent fire breaks. Now there were no distant views at all. Back in May, we walked through similar valleys in oppressive heat and really struggled to keep going. In October, the weather was still warm but thankfully the stifling temperatures of the summer were no more.

At last, the landscape opened out to reveal views of the distant Fóia, at 902 metres the highest mountain in the Serra de Monchique and, in fact, the whole Algarve. Day 10 of the Via Algarviana sees hikers heading up and over the summit of the lower neighbouring peak of Picota before descending to Monchique. Fóia itself is not tackled until Day 11 – and even then the Via Algarviana route does not actually climb to the busy summit (though the website insists 'the visit is mandatory').

This time, we approached the Algarve's highest peak along a zigzagging path through aroma-filled eucalyptus forests. The foliage was green and lush, a reminder that it rains far more in the mountains than on the coast. Everywhere there was ample evidence of the soil's fertility, from the crops in the fields to the abundance of pomegranate, lemon and orange trees. Here in the hills, the cork trees were larger than the ones we'd encountered further south and would provide shade from the summer sun.

In the 'saddle' that lies between Fóia and Picota, the air felt fresher and, dare-I-say-it, more than a little nippy. We passed a dry stream, a solitary horse, lots of expensive-looking villas and a lake. After hours of gradual climbing, we were growing weary and were frustrated when, every now and then, our route plunged briefly downhill before continuing its relentless upwards trajectory.

Eventually we emerged from the wooded path to follow an old lane dotted with traditional houses and well-tended terraced gardens. Maybe it was my imagination, but as I wandering past in my shorts, a rucksack strapped to my back, I sensed I was drawing considerable attention – and even the occasional disapproving look – from some of the older village women who were covered from head to toe.

Harri had booked us into the same hotel as last time. We hadn't been hugely impressed with the Miradoura da Serro and the customer service left a lot to be desired; however, given the scant choice of affordable hotel accommodation in Monchique we were prepared to give it a second chance. We trudged up the hill (a hotel with *miradoura* in its name has to be located on a hill), amused by the plonking of a tatty leather settee on the pavement almost directly opposite rows of exquisitely handcrafted 'scissor chairs'.

These 'scissor chairs' probably date back to Roman times and their current-day creator is a local man José Leonardo Salvador, one of the few remaining carpenters with the skills to make them.

On our second visit to Monchique, we had no trouble locating the hotel's unmarked entrance door next to a small supermarket. At reception, we were greeted more warmly than on our first visit (perhaps because we were now aware this hotel demands guests hand over the exact money *in cash* and obliged) and we were allocated a good-sized room at the back of the building with great views of the surrounding mountains from the tiny terrace. The furniture was as sparse as ever, and there had been no rush to furnish the rooms with modern televisions, but on the whole the accommodation was as good as one could expect for the price (€45 including breakfast).

Besides, we had no intention of hanging around our hotel room. All day we'd been salivating about our evening meal. On our first visit to Monchique, we'd walked into an unpromising-looking cafe called O Ze and unearthed the most delicious Portuguese cuisine. We knew exactly what we would be eating tonight: *steak au poivre*. We're not big meat eaters, preferring chicken and fish at home, but this dish at O Ze is not to be missed.

Last time, the winds had picked up and the mountain air was so cold there was barely a soul on the streets. Tonight, with the hurricane yet to arrive, local people were making the most of the warm, autumn evening. As a consequence, the café was packed full and we were lucky to get a table.

We had planned to drink white wine with our meal (I don't like red); however, the café owner had other ideas and recommended, via his English-speaking daughter, that we try *vinho verde*. We did ... while in Rome and all that ... and were immediately hooked on this slightly effervescent but non-sparkling wine.

The literal translation of the name is somewhat misleading. *Vinho verde* is not a 'green wine' but a young wine drunk just three to six months after the grapes are harvested. The wine originates from the Vinho Verde region in northern Portugal and makes up 9% of the country's total output.

Strictly speaking, tonight wasn't really the first time I'd drunk 'young wine'. Back in the late seventies, my dad – a man who liked his hobbies and worked his way through many – decided to take up wine-making. In the year or two that followed, he produced all manner of interesting tipples, including elderberry, blackberry and even rice wine. Unhappily for him (though not for me), dad's newfound passion coincided with one of my own teenage interests ... drinking!

Back at our hotel, clever Harri managed to get the ancient portable television working and we spent an enjoyable half hour making up ludicrous dialogue for a Portuguese soap with cardboard-looking sets even less convincing than the ones in the original series of British soap *Crossroads*. There was worse. Knowing those wobbling walls would destroy any illusion of reality for viewers, the producers had interjected the same aerial shot of moving traffic between studio-shot scenes.

As I groaned at the hammy acting, stock external shots and everything else, Harri couldn't resist his usual jibes about *Coronation Street*. Wouldn't someone from Portugal view my favourite soap as unfavourably as I was viewing theirs, he asked. How could that happen? I demanded, reminding him *Corrie*'s favourite sets – the Rovers Return, Roy's Rolls and Streetcars – are extremely realistic, the writing/dialogue is superb and the acting second to none. Sorry Portuguese soap lovers, but there is just no comparison.

For photographs visit <u>uk.pinterest.com/thewalkerswife</u>

DAY 5: MARMELETE TO ALJEZUR

Hurricane Joaquin swept across the Atlantic and hit the west coast of Portugal a few hours earlier than anticipated. At the Miradoura da Serro, Harri was awoken by the ferocity of the rain. He rushed onto our terrace to dismantle three makeshift washing lines and the clothes that were supposed to be drying overnight *before the rains came*. In the darkness – and his haste – he left behind four soon-to-be-saturated sports socks.

Overnight, the landscape had changed beyond recognition. Yesterday, we'd stood at the window gazing out across terracotta rooftops and wooded mountain slopes. Twelve hours later, Monchique was engulfed in low-lying cloud, with torrential rain sweeping across the *serra*. Dismayed, we realised how desperately we had wanted the forecast to be wrong, or maybe just not as bad as predicted.

Over breakfast we debated our options. Pre-Joaquin our plan had been to walk from Monchique to Marmelete where we would join the Via Algarviana link route to Aljezur, a reasonable distance of around 18.6km, but one described in the official guide as *'difficil'*. What's more, Marmelete was over 10km from here, meaning we'd have that additional distance to cover too. We wouldn't normally flinch at a 30km hiking day, but the storm was showing no sign of abating. Our waterproofs were light and intended for showers not hurricane-originating Atlantic storms. We would be drenched before we reached the outskirts of Monchique.

Harri suggested we take a taxi to Marmelete and walk from there. He'd written up detailed route instructions from Monchique to Marmelete when we walked the Via Algarviana so there was nothing to be gained by walking the route again. After that, however, we had no choice. Harri wanted to include the alternative finish via Aljezur and the Rota Vicentina (GR11) in his forthcoming hiking guidebook and he couldn't do that if we didn't walk the route ourselves, starting with the Marmelete to Aljezur section.

In fact, when I say we were discussing all this over breakfast, I use the word 'breakfast' loosely. We were, in fact, sitting at our breakfast table in the hotel's dining room at the agreed time, yet there was no indication that breakfast was about to be served. Just like on our last visit to the Miradouro da Serra, *mein* hosts appeared completely unconcerned that guests – their *paying* guests – were sat in the dining room twiddling their thumbs while they were ... well, presumably twiddling their thumbs elsewhere in the building.

We heaved a sigh of relief when we eventually heard footsteps on the stairs, only to discover the newcomer had come to *eat* breakfast, not to serve it. We got talking and it transpired this Dutch lady had lived nearby for many years until her family persuaded her to return to Holland (a decision we suspected she had come to regret). She told us how she returned to Monchique regularly to catch up with old friends and maintain her links with a country she adored.

When breakfast did eventually arrive, it was a pretty disappointing offering. White bread rolls, sliced ham (of the unappetising kind), sliced cheese (ditto), honey and thickly-sliced marmalade. There was no fruit, yoghurt, jam or juice to be seen. Have these hoteliers been learning their customer service skills from dubbed episodes of *Fawlty Towers*?

The food may have been basic, but the breakfast room conversation was enjoyable. The Dutch lady told us she'd lived on the hillside below Fóia for 18 years and had loved the relaxed way of life in Portugal, especially the abundance of fruit and vegetables. When her husband died, she remained in Monchique for another 13 years, until her own health problems – and the size/layout of her hillside property – forced her to evaluate her life in rural Algarve. She returned to Holland, but hates the hectic pace of live in her native country and spends as much time in Portugal as possible.

Her words reminded me of an interesting article I once read, when the author had pointed out that once you leave your home town/country it can never *quite* be your home again. In the intervening period both you and the place you left will change, and the people you have left behind will move on with their lives. It's a sobering thought and perhaps one worth considering for those of us with wanderlust.

When I first returned to Newport in the eighties after having worked in Cornwall for nearly three years, I certainly felt at odds with the town I'd called home. Though family and friends welcomed me back with open arms, for that first year I really struggled to settle. It wasn't that I wanted to go back to Cornwall, just that the experience of living somewhere different had changed my perception of everything. For a long time, I felt disorientated and rootless. There was nowhere that felt like home, nowhere I wanted to be. It was only when I met my first husband and started a family that I was able to silence that restless voice in my head, albeit temporarily.

With hindsight – and the passing of several decades – I wonder if it was in fact cowardice that pulled me back to my industrial birthplace that autumn. The same fear of the unknown, the uncomfortable, that ties so many of us to jobs, places, even relationships. For it certainly wasn't any affinity with or love for Newport that persuaded me spend the next thirty years of my life in the city. This was only our third visit to mainland Portugal, and – just like the Dutch lady – I already knew I'd found my spiritual home

As hikers, we might not have been overly enthusiastic about the arrival of Hurricane Joaquin, but the torrential downpour was undoubtedly being greeted with relief by the Bombeiros Portugueses, who are charged with fighting hundreds of forest fires each year. I'd been astonished to learn many of fire stations across Portugal are manned entirely by volunteers, like the Royal National Lifeboat Institution in the UK. These brave and dedicated individuals regularly risk their lives for no financial recompense.

In the UK, it's always struck me as anomalous that those who courageously set out in perilous seas for the purpose of saving lives are not accorded the same financial worth as those emergency service personnel who work on land. While the police and fire officers receive salaries and reasonable pension arrangements, the RNLI's volunteers respond day and night, and risking life and limb without payment. Like the RNLI, Portugal's volunteer *bombeiros* are respected and admired by all; however, the idea that altruism should be sufficient reward for acts of tremendous courage (and even death) seems wrong.

Only the previous week, nearly 200 fire-fighters from across the Algarve joined the GNR (part of Portugal's military) to tackle a huge fire near Marmelete, which rapidly split and moved in different directions. They were assisted by four aircraft and a helicopter, which gives some idea of the enormity of the fast-moving fire.

Judging from the sound of the rain outside, the Algarve's bombeiros could expect a quiet day today. The hotel wasn't particularly welcoming, but right then I'd have done anything to linger in our room all day. Just thinking about the conditions that awaited us outside was enough to make me shiver.

When the Dutch lady mentioned there was a daily bus from Monchique to Marmelete, we didn't need persuading. Harri had already written up his guidebook instructions to Marmelete so it didn't matter if we cut the day's walking short and just covered the stretch from Marmelete to Aljezur. With the rain expected to continue until late afternoon, there was no avoiding it, but at least this way we cut shorten our ordeal by about two hours.

Our first stop was the tourist information centre in the middle of Monchique. We'd called here in May, when the young woman had been extremely helpful. Her English was excellent and it was she who told us about the community centre enterprise when we'd been struggling to find accommodation in Marmelete.

We could barely disguise our delight when we spotted her behind the desk. Yes, she confirmed, there was indeed a bus from Monchique to Marmelete; however, it didn't leave town until 12 noon. She gave us directions to the bus stop and we reluctantly headed out into the rain again to check its whereabouts.

Locating the bus stop was straightforward enough; however, Harri wanted to triple-check we were in the right place so we asked the young man who was waiting there. Whether he misunderstood our question, his English was not sufficiently fluent or he was mischief-making good and proper, he told us 'no' this was not the right place and pointed down the road opposite. We thanked him – with hindsight, perhaps a good, sharp kick would have been better – and wandered off through the downpour to find the 'right' bus stop. By now we were absolutely soaked, despite having done nothing but wander around the centre of Monchique.

No matter how hard we searched, we were unable to find another bus stop. In desperation, we returned to the tourist information office and asked the young woman if she could draw us a map. Surprise, surprise, we'd been at the right bus stop all along.

Now resembling two drowned rats, we headed to the wonderful Loja do Chocolate e Cha Magico, an amazing gift shop we discovered last time around, which sells delicious homemade fudge.

Lisa, the shop's Welsh owner, was as friendly as ever when I bought my double portion of maple and walnut fudge, but showed no indication of recognising us from our previous visit. We're clearly not as memorable as we like to think!

Being British, it wasn't long before we got talking about the weather. The current downpour was the first rain of any significance since April and, as a result, was much welcomed by the locals, if not visiting hikers. It could of course be hearsay, but Lisa told us last week's forest fire had been started by a Portuguese man who had bought a house near Fóia and rather fecklessly decided to clear the land around his house ... by setting light to it. From the ferocity of the fire and the reports I've read, I'm assuming his property is no more.

The talk of misadventure soon had Lisa recounting her own fire horror story. It was August 2003 and forest fires raged across Central Portugal and the Algarve, ravaging everything in their wake. Over 35,000 hectares of forestry was destroyed by flames between August 7 and 12. Then, just when local people were thinking the worst was over, another devastating fire took hold in the Serra de Monchique, this time burning hundreds of square kilometres of forestry over a ten-day period.

The *bombeiros* worked around the clock to keep the fires under control; however, the propensity of profitable (and highly flammable) eucalyptus plantations in the region meant they were always going to struggle. Lisa, like many other local residents, lost everything in the Great Fóia Fire of 2003 and 21 people, including two fire fighters, died. As our planet continues to heat up things are only likely to get worse.

One ecologist estimates that '10% of the Portuguese state has gone up in smoke in less than a generation'. The vast eucalyptus plantations across the country (roughly a quarter of Portugal's forested land) exacerbate the problem by drawing moisture from the dry ground and displacing indigenous trees like the relatively fire-resistant cork oak. Small abandoned plots of land with absent owners, where dead vegetation is not cleared from the ground, only makes things worse.

The horrific fires in Central Portugal in June 2017 which left 64 people dead and more than 200 injured have in part led to the introduction of new laws to limit eucalyptus planting (the forest reform legislation was already being discussed at the time of the Pedragão Grande fires but the vote came after the fires). The law, which comes into effect in February 2018, will prohibit the planting of the invasive species in areas greater than half a hectare (roughly one and a quarter acres). This doesn't sound like a huge step forward in fire prevention to me; however, Portugal is one of Europe's biggest exporters of pulp and paper and, as we are only too aware, a country's economy must always come first.

All this talk of fire and blazes made the heavy rainfall feel more like a blessing than a problem ... until we bade farewell to Lisa and stepped outside to wade back to the bus stop. It was nearly noon, our clothes were soaked through and we still hadn't started the day's hiking.

Finally it was noon and the Marmelete bus arrived. It didn't seem like we were going anywhere fast though, for no sooner had we paid our fares than our driver got off. Assuming he was heading discretely to the gents, we were surprised to see him bending over and gathering chestnuts (*castanheiro*) from the wet pavement.

Monchique is the only place in the Algarve where chestnuts grow and the town holds an annual Chestnut Festival in November. On one of our visits to Madeira, I remember walking in the mountains and scooping up freshly-fallen chestnuts from the trail. Maybe the similarity in fauna explains why the Serra de Monchique landscape reminds us of Madeira.

The locals had clearly decided to sit Joaquin out at home, for there was only one passenger on the bus besides us. She disembarked a short distance from Monchique and for the remainder of the journey, it was just Harri and me. In the relative warmth of the bus, I couldn't stop shivering; I certainly envied anyone who had the option of staying indoors today.

When the bus eventually pulled up outside the community centre at Marmelete it was all I could do to drag myself to the door. Thankfully the air outside was warm, though that was little consolation as I contemplated the 18.6km of wet-weather hiking ahead of us and shuddered.

At Monchique's tourist information office, we'd enquired about the current status of Marmelete's community centre/hiking hostel project and were advised that work was 'progressing', although as yet there remained no bedding for overnight visitors. The obvious *lack of progress* made wonder if many Via Algarviana hikers had made use of the basic facilities during the summer months. I was just grateful we wouldn't need a 'bed' in Marmelete this time around!

Most of today's walking was on forestry tracks and there was rather more climbing than I'd anticipated on what was a predominantly downhill trajectory. For the umpteenth time, I thanked my lucky stars that we'd packed our waterproofs, even though we hadn't expected to need them until we stepped off the plane back home.

In fine weather, there are magnificent panoramic views from these mountain tracks; now, a thick mist obscured everything except our immediate surroundings.

We trudged on, the walking made even more tiresome by the heavy, sodden clay which clung so determinedly to the soles of our shoes that it took enormous effort to walk at even a half-decent speed. And if the uphill sections were physically tough, the slippery downhill trails demanded our full attention just to remain upright.

While I fretted about how I would ever get my shoes clean again, Harri was more concerned about our devices, particularly the digital voice recorder and iPad. After the scare in Snowdonia when the first had got so wet he'd been unable to switch it off, Harri was again concerned that our essential technical equipment would baulk at the unexpected turn in the weather. Everything was packed in plastic bags, however, as we knew from experience, those tiny H_2O molecules have a way of penetrating even the most watertight packaging.

If being wet and cold wasn't bad enough, the big toe on my right foot had pushed through the fabric of my sock and as a result was being strangulated. I'd be walking sockless at this rate – it was the second pair to lose the battle with the same big toe this week.

We reached the shallow Cerca stream and I waded across without as much as a murmur of dissent, my feet no wetter when I reached the distant bank than before. Despite our discomfort, it was hard not to be impressed by the lush beauty of the landscape. Every now and then we'd glimpse isolated properties half-concealed by vegetation and wonder who the people were who chose to live here in the mountains.

The rain was less relentless now and there were even moments when it stopped altogether. We'd find ourselves peering up at the shifting clouds, only to have our hopes cruelly dashed minutes later with an even heavier downpour. It was getting harder and harder to stay positive, despite Harri's insistence that it was going to stop raining ... eventually.

We were within a stone's throw of Aljezur by the time it eventually stopped raining and the first tiny specks of blue began to appear in what had previously been solid cloud. This was our first time on the west coast proper since we holidayed in Setúbal in 2011 and I'd really been looking forward to our overnight stop at Aljezur.

From our lofty vantage point in the hills overlooking the town, the castle that Aljezur is so famous for – generally described as enjoying a commanding position over the town – looked to be perched atop a molehill. Aljezur was bigger than I'd expected. It was green and appealing, with a wide flood plain alongside the river and rows of whitewashed housing on a distant hillside. Despite the proximity of the ocean – just out of sight over a ridge – there was little indication that the town was close to the coast.

Making the most of the brighter weather, we stopped for the obligatory beers in a square next to the church where we were entertained by the antics of several local dogs.

We had high expectations of Vicentina Aparthotel, in part because it had a four star rating, but mostly because we were paying considerably more to stay there than we'd paid for almost any other place in Algarve *ever*.

On the plus side, the room shouted 'interior designer' in that way that boutique hotels always do and there was Wi-Fi and a powerful hairdryer which was most useful for drying my soaked-through Brasher sandals. The shower was excellent and the huge bed was incredibly comfortable. I got ridiculously excited when I found the BBC World News channel on the television. Our balcony was pretty naff – it was tiny, overlooked the main road and boasted two grey plastic chairs next to a bulky generator on the wall – but this hardly mattered given that we'd had enough 'outside' for one day.

The big downside was that the hotel was located slightly away from the main thrust of things and its restaurant was closed despite it being Saturday night. This was most frustrating; we rarely eat in hotels (too expensive), but after the day we'd experienced we had agreed to push the boat out – going out in search of food *in wet boots* had felt like too much much effort. Now, it seemed, we had no choice.

Despite feeling shattered, we showered, dressed in clean clothes and set off to look for somewhere to eat. Walking around Aljezur at night is a pleasure – the town is well-lit and the traffic surprisingly light. There didn't seem to be much life in the area around the hotel – unless you count the supermarket next door – so we headed across the river to the historic enclaves.

The first establishment we came across was bursting at the seams. Compared to last night's meal in Monchique, the menu also looked a little pricey. We decided to keep looking and soon arrived at another restaurant. This time there were plenty of empty tables, which aroused our suspicions. We debated what to do – wait patiently for a seat to become available in the other venue (because surely thirty people can't be wrong) or take a risk and eat within the hour in an empty restaurant.

We studied the menu in the window. It appeared identical in content and price to the other one so, driven by hunger and exhaustion, we decided to go inside. Despite the obvious lack of clientele – for which we could fathom no reason except perhaps a local vendetta – the food was excellent. Harri chose fried squid and I stuck to my usual chicken piri piri. The service and ambience were good and there was no-one hovering in the doorway, giving us the evil eye as we lingered over our glasses of port. With wine, the bill came to €32, considerably pricier than last night, but still a snip compared to eating out in the UK.

For photographs visit uk.pinterest.com/thewalkerswife

DAY 6: ALJEZUR TO ARRIFANA

For the second morning running, the breakfast service fell short. The buffet-style offerings were already laid out – including a rather nice fruit salad – but we generally look for our caffeine fix first and there was no sign of any coffee or tea-making facilities.

After two visits, we now expect shoddy customer service from the Miradoura da Serra; however, the Vicentina Aparthotel is a four star boutique establishment and I wasn't going anywhere until I'd had my cup of *chá*.

Eventually, a female member of staff meandered into the kitchen area – presumably to grab herself a mug of something hot – and I raced across the dining room and pounced on her. She wasn't a waitress, but she did kindly organise some hot water for us.

I remember reading a long, long time ago that you know you're getting old when you begin to feel at odds with the world around you. I got to that point at least a decade ago and these days I frequently feel so at odds with modern life I find myself shouting 'I don't believe it!' more often than Victor Meldrew. This morning I pondered why a smallish hotel in a town of around 6,000 should think it more important to have a beauty salon on the premises than to provide guests with tea and coffee at breakfast. You could die of thirst waiting there in the breakfast room, but all the hotel website seems concerned about are the 'nervous terminals' of your skin and whether you choose a 'half-hour spotted massage' or the full hour. Okay, that last observation is a bit unfair ... like most sites (including my own website thewalkerswife.co.uk) the site is translated automatically resulting in the customary but highly entertaining gobbledegook. You get the idea though ... 'Unbe-lieeeve-able!'

We sipped our tea and looked out on the swimming pool and beyond to the multi-storey car park of the adjacent Intermerché supermarket. It must be said, it wasn't one of the prettiest backdrops we've seen from hotel grounds.

At least it had stopped raining and, for the time being, the weather seemed relatively settled albeit a little greyer than we'd have liked. Soon after leaving Marmelete, we'd parted company with the Via Algarviana to follow the link route to Aljezur; we would not see the familiar red and white waymarking again until almost the end of our trip.

One of the reasons we'd returned to the Algarve so soon after finishing the Via Algarviana was to try out an alternative route to Cabo de São Vicente. Harri's plan was for us to follow some of the hiking trails which are collectively known as the Rota Vicentina. From Aljezur, we'd be following the Historical Way until somewhere between Vila do Bispo and Cabo de São Vicente, after which we would join the 'demanding and only to be done on foot' Fishermen's Trail.

But first, we had a Moorish castle to explore. As we discovered yesterday, the town of Aljezur is really two distinct settlements divided by a wide level valley (and a river). Our hotel and the majority of the town's civic amenities are located in the newer of these settlements, Igreja Nova ('new church'), which was built in the decades following the devastating earthquake of 1755 at the behest of the Bishop of the Algarve. At the time, malaria (and death) was rife in the old quarter and the Bishop thought people would be more willing to leave if they didn't have to go far!

I was more at risk of foot rot this morning ... or I would have been if I'd put my usual shoes on. Despite my best efforts with the hairdryer, the insides were still sodden. I couldn't face setting off with wet feet so I fished out my old Brasher sandals, now in their ninth year and still going strong.

We retraced last night's route, crossing the Aljezur river from modern town to historic enclaves on a narrow bridge. There was a sign explaining that this metal monstrosity hadn't always been here, but that the nearby medieval bridge was swept away by floods in March 1947 (the same time melting snow was causing widespread flooding across the UK).

Gazing down at the shallow trickle of water running over the silted riverbed, it was hard to believe there was a time when Aljezur had been a thriving port, the only safe haven for ships along between Alcácer do Sol on the Atlantic coast and Sagres. Before the valley silted up, boats arrived here from Lisbon and Tavira, from northern France and Spain.

Trade was brisk, with cloth, fruit, vegetables, spices, honey, olive oil, dried fruit and even medicinal plants changing hands.

Then, the Aljezur river flowed so strongly it powered local mills, and flour was exported to Portuguese colonies in Africa. Fishing boats chugged down the river, returning with catches that included tuna, mackerel, hake, sardines, octopus, bass and conger eel.

Like most of the Iberian Peninsula, Algarve (*Gharb Al-Andalus* or simply *Al-Gharb*) was under Moorish rule for five centuries. And it was these Islamic invaders who were responsible for the impressive castles which dominate the landscape nearly one thousand years later.

Despite involving a short detour, Aljezur castle was, we felt, worth a quick visit. There was no entrance fee, which meant we wouldn't be compelled to hang around reading every last interpretation board to get our money's worth.

The steep ascent up a narrow, tiled road would have been pleasant had we not needed to leap aside every few minutes for a carload of sightseers to speed past. After this had happened four or five times, I started getting irritated. 'I don't believe it!' I shouted at a retreating vehicle. Okay, there was a black cloud overhead and it had just started to spot with rain, but does it never cross anyone else's mind that a brisk, ten-minute walk might actually do them the world of good? Settling comfortably into the moral high ground, I considered how the lazy human race might one day lose its legs altogether, just as the slow-moving aquatic manatee had done. And whose fault would that be, eh?

By the time we reached the top of the hill, the rain had stopped. I tried not to glare at those visitors who had whizzed past us on the way up, snapped the obligatory photographs and were already rushing back to their parked cars, presumably to drive at full pelt to the next 'must-see' tourist site.

The views from the castle were panoramic and well worth the detour. Whichever direction you gazed there was something to feast your eyes upon: the rolling, wooded hills we'd already walked, the gleaming white properties of Igreja Nova and the fertile plains beyond.

From here we had a much better view of the meandering river. With the natural defences of location and the far-reaching and unobstructed views of the surrounding area, Aljezur's castle served an important function in defending the town from attacks by Barbary pirates. Unsurprisingly, this castle was the last in Algarve to be conquered by the Christians, with victory finally claimed at dawn on 24 June 1249.

We wandered around the fortifications, clambering onto the steep earth mound in the centre where the Portuguese flag was flying and enjoying the juxtaposition of lush, verdant hills and towering stone walls. We took photographs of dare-devils walking the length of those walls and perused the interpretation boards. There were several points of architectural interest – two massive towers and a cistern – but it's hard to impress a Welsh woman where castles are concerned.

Speaking of flags, Aljezur Castle is one of seven former Moorish fortifications reputedly represented on the Portuguese national flag. The current flag with its green and red background was introduced in 1911, months after the Portuguese monarchy was overthrown and the country became a republic. The seven yellow castles – portrayed as identical on the flag – symbolise Portugal's victories over the Moors under Afonso III (though the number of castles shown on the flag is likely arbitrary).

Now that the Aljezur river is unnavigable the people in these parts have turned their attention from fish to sweet potatoes. No-one seems to know why or when the *batata doce* was introduced to Aljezur, but a legend tells of how a stew containing the Aljezur sweet potato gave the Christian knights the strength to overthrow the Moors and regain control of the castle after nearly three hundred years. Sadly, like many other legends, this one is unlikely to be true. Records suggest that Portugal's explorers did not introduce the sweet potato to Portugal until the 17th century.

What intrigues me about the long, twisted sweet potatoes in Algarve's supermarkets here was their uncanny resemblance to the meandering 'arms' of the region's many reservoirs.

So enamoured are the people of Aljezur with the yellow flesh of their sweet potato that they hold an annual festival in its honour. The Aljezur sweet potato is used in many local recipes and has even been officially recognised as a product with a protected designation of origin (like Cornish pasties and champagne).

At the 2017 festival, a sweet potato beer was launched. The aptly named 'Tuber Bock' supposedly has a 'malty flavour' and is claimed by its brewers to be the perfect accompaniment to grilled meats, stews, sausages and cheeses. It sounds like the perfect brew to enjoy at Querença's next sausage festival.

After fifteen minutes, we decided to leave the tourists to it and followed a winding path through yet more eucalyptus forests. At a T-junction of tracks, a signpost gave us the choice of walking directly to Arrifana (8km) or taking the alternative coastal route (14km). No prices for guessing which trail we'd be following.

I was just enjoying the level walking when I spotted something I generally try to avoid at all costs – a very large bull. In the UK, almost all farmland is surrounded by high hedging or fencing, but here in Algarve there are fewer concerns about passersby straying onto land where livestock are grazing. Unless I was mistaken, it appeared nothing was separating our onward track and the grassland where the massive marauding beast stood. I instinctively slowed down, casting my eyes around for possible escape routes.

Harri grew up on a dairy farm and is far more confident around bulls than I am. He reckons most bulls are reluctant to abandon their dairy cows for the sole purpose of charging a bunch of walkers, however much they stamp their hooves and glower at us. Personally, I'd prefer not to risk annoying the one bull in a hundred that *is* prepared to charge us. As we grew close, we could see that a single line of twine marked the perimeter of the field. This seemed a spectacularly inadequate deterrent to stop an angry bull, but thankfully it seemed to do the trick. As we passed – far too close for comfort – the animal made no attempt to leave his bell-decorated harem. It seemed Harri had been right ... *again*.

The next few hours were hilly and generally tough going. Fortunately, the weather had taken a turn for the better and the sun was shining again even if the ground was still problematic. Yesterday's rainfall had created rivulets in the clay tracks, which didn't pose a problem on flatter terrain, but made it difficult when we encountered any really steep section. Then, every time I planted my foot down, I felt the earth move and had to concentrate on keeping my balance. I continued the uphill trudge, expecting to go sliding down the hill at any moment. Typically, Harri didn't seem to be having any problem and I found myself falling farther and farther behind.

We passed a development of several villas and smaller houses where we were shocked to see that the larger of the villas had had what looked like oil or tar poured over its beautifully constructed stone walls. I was saddened that an act of such deliberate destruction had occurred in these tranquil surroundings. Until now, we'd seen little evidence of vandalism, although graffiti is ubiquitous in the Algarve and frequently political. In particular, the constant scrawling of WASP across buildings, railway stations, fences, etc, had intrigued us. At first I wondered if WASP was in fact Portugal's very own Banksy? It's rumoured that the infamous but still-unidentified English graffiti artist once said, 'If you don't own a train company then you go and paint on one instead'.

I've since read that WASP is more likely a street protest against the 'White Anglo Saxon Protestants' who are increasingly flocking to the Algarve and driving up house prices. I wondered if the large single-storey villa had been defaced for political reasons or whether it was just mindless vandalism, or even if it matters when the result is the same.

The scent of the fire-loving eucalyptus trees wafted through the air and the views down the valley to Amoreira opened out. Just as we were getting our first tantalising glimpse of the sea, Harri steered me to the left and we headed inland again, frustrating any thoughts I'd been nurturing of a late morning plunge into those foaming Atlantic waves (of course, I'm joking!).

We settled down for elevenses outside an abandoned farmhouse that was missing its windows, doors and large sections of its roof, but would have been perfect for renovation had there been better road access. My Via Algarviana-initiated obsession with ants now well-established, I amused myself by dropping small pieces of crisps onto the ground and watching a succession of lone ants lift the proportionately enormous pieces of food onto their backs then scuttling off with them. Where these crisp crumbs would end up, I had no idea, but it was clear that in the ant world finders are not keepers. The first ant on the scene would have immediately released a message (via pheromones) saying something like 'Hey, come over here, I've found food,' and the remainder of the nest would be on the spot within minutes.

I was so absorbed in watching the crisp convoy that it took Harri to alert me to the fact that one group of about eight ants were carrying something far more recently *alive* than fried potatoes. I watched with fascination as the relatively tiny ants rushed past my feet with what appeared to be the inert body of a (presumably dead) dragon fly. These tireless workers now had the basis for their evening meal; meat and potatoes.

Ants aside, we were fascinated with the tightly coiled zebra-striped springy things we kept seeing on the track. Closer inspection revealed them to be millipedes (they are the ones with two pairs of legs per body segment ... centipedes have only one pair and are flatter-looking).

Our meandering route gradually steered us towards the ocean and soon we could hear the thunderous waves pummelling the cliffs below and taste the salt in the air. It's no wonder this stretch of coast – so reminiscent of rugged north Cornwall – is popular with surfers.

Tonight's base was Arrifana Retreat, a rather nice villa/guest house in the urbanisation of Vale de Telha, run by keen surfers Kate and Stimpy. The couple clearly have plenty of energy because as well as welcoming guests into their beautiful modern villa, they also run a surf school and have two small children, Flynn and baby Mya.

We intended to explore Arrifana itself in due course, but as the villa was en route it made sense to offload our rucksacks first. The door was opened by Stimpy, who – and I'm sure he won't mind me saying this – is the original article where beach dudes are concerned. Within minutes Kate had arrived on the scene and was offering us tea and cake. Soon we were all sitting around the kitchen table, enjoying liberal servings of banana cake and chatting away like old friends. The couple run the guest house in what Harri and I think is the perfect way. There are no set meal times, no additional costs for pack lunch and no bar, just a fridge stocked full of delicious food that you can help yourself to at will. There was even beer and wine, though they do ask for one euro per beer/glass of wine. As the nearest proper supermarket is in Aljezur, we thought this was a lovely thoughtful gesture, particularly for outdoor types like us who don't necessarily who don't necessarily have our own transport.

Our triple-bedded room was bright and modern with a decent-sized en suite and a large private veranda with sea views, seating and plenty of space for Harri to put up his clothes line. The whole package cost just €54, a mere snip for such delightful surroundings and thoughtful, friendly hosts.

Feeling refreshed after our afternoon snack, it wasn't long before we were setting off to explore Arrifana itself. The housing runs along the clifftop, with one steep road leading to the beach and a second to the little harbour. Like many surfing resorts, there is not a huge amount to see except the beach and those massive, sand-pummelling waves.

Those waves might be magnet for surfers worldwide, but they pose a serious concern to the country's environmentalists. Portugal's entire Atlantic coast, in particular the Algarve region and the area around Lisbon, is threatened by erosion as climate change causes sea levels to rise and storms to become more frequent (and violent). Beaches on the west coast are retreating too, in some instances by up to a few metres a year, as fierce storms and natural changes in wave directions take their toll. Intriguingly, much of the sand stripped from the west coast is carried by the ocean to the beaches of the Algarve.

There were huge storm clouds gathering overhead. If we wanted to explore Arrifana, we needed to get a move on. We walked the short distance to the ocean and headed towards the Ponta da Atalaia – perhaps a little faster than was wise, because within minutes of passing some traditional fishermen's cottages we found ourselves being chased by a gaggle of seven very scary geese. A local woman appeared at a doorway to find out what the racket was all about. I don't know if you can call off geese in the way you can dogs who are misbehaving, but this lady made no attempt to control the crazed birds and just stood there on her doorstep chuckling.

Terrified I might have been, but I remained professional to the end. Even as I ran for my life, I continued to snap away, thus demonstrating my fearless dedication as a wildlife photographer!

On the subject of geese, this stretch of coast is renowned for the abundance of goose barnacles, a seafood delicacy we have yet to taste. The species thrives on coastal rocks in choppy seas which make their harvesting a risky business ... though maybe not as dangerous as trying to get past their winged namesakes.

Having escaped with our legs – and our lives – we strolled through a restored stone archway to gaze at the wild, rugged coastline with its crashing waves, all the while keeping an eye on that darkening sky.

Arrifana's fortress was built in 1635 and was the first fortified point along this stretch of coast. Like so many of Portugal's monuments, it was destroyed in the 1755 earthquake. The parish priest at the time, Martin Pereira da Silva reported 'here the sea collected 30 fathoms and forth three times, inveighed against the walls of the fortress with such momentum, destroyed the gorge, and the structures, standing only the battery and walled curtain of the entrance door' (thank you Google translate).

Because of its important strategic position, the fortress was quickly rebuilt – and again destroyed by the sea. It seems the structure was eventually abandoned in the early nineteenth century and only the remains of the entrance walls and the doorway were mentioned in official reports for many decades.

In 1940, the powers that be in the Portuguese navy decided the site had no historic or cultural merit and sold it. Fortunately, this wasn't the nail in the coffin for the fortress and four years later the Commission of the Maritime Public Domain assumed responsibility for the site. The obvious renovations and improvements to access were made in 2011.

The fortress isn't the only important historic site on these clifftops. Portugal's only identified *ribát* – a twelfth-century hybrid between a fortress and a monastery – lies just one kilometre north of Arrifana.

In their academic paper, archaeologists Roma and Mário Varela Gomes write how the site – where the Moors hatched their battle plans in the final years of their occupation of Algarve – was known to exist from centuries-old writings, but was not discovered by them in 2001 (it gained National Portuguese Monument status in 2013). Three mosques were among the ruined buildings excavated here.

Built around 1130, the Ribát de Arrifana was only occupied for two decades and was abandoned for good after its founder Ibn Qasi was assassinated in Silves in 1151.

Fearing we were likely to get caught in a storm if we lingered too long, we took a few photographs and hastily departed from what must be one of the most photographed arches on this stretch of coastline.

We headed downhill and past the cottages, where I was relieved to see the geese had gone. We agreed Arrifana is an interesting place, a mixture of pristine, modern villas – including a house that had been designed to look like it was sliding down the sloping plot (at least we hoped the angle of the roof was intentional) – and traditional, single-storey houses we suspected hadn't changed much in decades.

We stopped for a drink at one of Arrifana's numerous bars before wandering down the steep hill to the beach. To our inexperienced eye, there didn't seem to be a whole lot of surfing going on, just a lot of rubber-clad figures bobbing around in the shallows. A few years back, Harri and I were walking the South West Coast Path – a long-distance challenge we have yet to complete – when we happened upon the Boardmasters Surf Festival in Newquay. What an exhilarating spectacle it was to witness those brave – some might say foolhardy – surfers riding the big waves. How terrifying it must be to see a wall of water powering towards you and knowing that you must pit your wits and very human body against the most powerful of the elements.

Here in Portugal, the very best surfers flock to Nazaré, north of Lisbon and about 350 kilometres from here. As the result of an underwater canyon less than one kilometre from the shore, Nazaré's Praia do Norte gets some of the largest waves in the world and attracts surfers whose fearlessness is matched only by their obsession.

There, eight-metre (26-foot) waves are normal, perhaps even considered a bit on the small size by the sport's big names. In November 2011, one giant wave secured a record for surfer Garrett McNamara – it was an incredible 23.8 metres (78-feet) high! The 2017 Big Wave Awards were dominated by Nazaré, with eleven of the forty worldwide nominations for surfing feats on the Portuguese coast.

The slate-coloured clouds blasting inland did not bode well for a balmy evening on our veranda. Sure enough, within minutes we were dashing back to the village to seek shelter from a very British-like downpour.

We headed for the nearest bar, uncertain how to adapt our plans to yet another change in weather. It was still too early to eat, but there seemed little sense in heading back to Arrifana Retreat – getting soaked in the process – only to come out again later for food.

The sense that we had somehow stumbled through a portal and arrived in Cornwall on a blustery autumn day continued when we chose the venue for our evening meal. Hello Sailor Restaurante is apparently German-owned, yet everything about the shabby chic furnishings, painted driftwood frames, and ubiquitous seashells shouted Cornwall. The restaurant didn't start serving food until 7pm and it was still only 6.30pm so we sat outside on bohemian, mismatched seating under a canopy with a bottle of our now-favourite *vinho verde*. Next to us two girls, who were clearly *serious* backpackers if the size of their rucksacks were anything to go by, sipped non-alcoholic drinks and persuaded their large, friendly Labrador that he'd prefer to lie under the table than make our acquaintance.

We'd polished off our first bottle by the time a member of staff came onto the veranda to call everyone inside. There were candles everywhere giving the room a warm, cosy ambience ... and making it very difficult to read the menu. When our meals arrived, we knew we'd chosen well for they were amazing. Harri had ordered the seafood spaghetti with clams, prawns and squid, while I opted for the gourmet burger. I think I gasped out loud when I saw the amount of food piled on our plates. These were hungry surfer portions and we'd done far fewer miles today than usual. Harri was also beginning to feel a little bit under the weather and was concerned he wouldn't be able to do his delicious food justice.

I felt fine, but the sheer quantity of food on my plate was mind-boggling. On closer inspection I realised my gourmet burger meal comprised an awful lot of food that didn't fall under the burger label – brown bread, fried egg, goat's cheese, a huge salad and an enormous portion of new potatoes. Seriously, I think we had enough food between us to feed six. The service was as good as the food and we were more than happy to pay the €45 bill, presented in a conch shell.

By the time we ventured outside again the rain had stopped and the evening air was pleasantly warm. Full of wine, food and goodwill, we agreed that overall we had enjoyed our brief visit to Arrifana.

Back at Arrifana Retreat, Harri surprised me by suddenly showing an interest in interior design.

'Why can't we have a bedroom like this?' he said, looking around at the plain white walls, the large three-section painting of sea, sky and sunset and the scarlet curtains over patio doors with a veranda beyond. We marvelled at how well everything had been put together, but then I thought about our own bedroom in a Victorian stone terrace.

Yes, the decor here was stylish and eye-catching; however, good design isn't just about importing a 'look' from one place to another. White walls, minimalist furnishings and tiled floors might work well in Algarve, but home in cold, damp Wales it's probably better to go for cosy, with rugs, candles ... and yes, even mismatched furnishings.

For photographs visit uk.pinterest.com/thewalkerswife

DAY 7: ARRIFANA TO CARRAPATEIRA

It had rained solidly overnight, possibly one of the reasons neither of us felt particularly rested this morning. Harri's mysterious malaise of the previous evening still lingered and I was getting conflicting messages from home about the state of my father's health. Add to the mix the two bottles of *vinho verde* we'd consumed at the Happy Sailor plus an earlier lager, and it was little wonder we weren't inclined to leap out of bed.

On the bright side, the rain had finally stopped ... for the time being at least. Harri had already checked the forecast and it seemed we should brace ourselves for another soaking later in the day. Since Monchique, the weather had felt more Wales than Algarve. Typically, around 80 mm of rain falls in this region throughout the entire month of October. Joaquin had a lot to answer for.

The breakfast arrangements at Arrifana Retreat suited us perfectly. Instead of seating guests down at a specific time and bringing food to the table, we were encouraged to roll into the kitchen at whatever time suited us and help ourselves to eggs, cheese, ham, several varieties of bread, fruit, yoghurt and cereal.

We were just tucking into a veritable feast when Kate appeared at the doorway and urged us to make sandwiches and take some fruit with us. Accustomed to catering for surfers as they are, this accommodating couple clearly understood that organising midday food can be difficult without transport. The nearest shop was a minimum 20-minute walk away in the nearby Vale da Telha urbanisation.

Kate chatted for a while, telling us how she and Stimpy had initially been drawn to the Algarve's west coast by their shared love of surfing and how setting up Arrifana Retreat and sharing their home with other outdoor types enabled them to live the life they had always dreamed about. It can't be easy juggling an accommodation business with two young children but if anyone can make it succeed, this delightful couple can. Thinking about our own long-term plans, we quizzed Kate about the practicalities of living in Portugal. Everything was mostly great, she told us, although her recent experience of giving birth in a small Portuguese hospital had highlighted a few language difficulties. Baby Mya was born with jaundice; however she was deemed fit to go home as long as Kate kept an eye on her

'Return to the hospital with Mya if she starts looking like a rabbit,' the obstetrician instructed a baffled Kate. It was only afterwards she realised the Portuguese doctor had confused the English words for carrot and rabbit. There was only cause for concern if her baby daughter's jaundice worsened to the extent that her skin looked orange – not if she developed buck teeth!

With the shopping trip no longer needed, we bade farewell to our lovely hosts and headed directly to the coast. Soon, we were standing on high cliffs gazing down at the slate-coloured Atlantic ocean. Along the reaches of the coast, endless waves crashed ashore with such ferocity that huge plumes of sea spray rose into the air, obscuring the cliffs. Our disappointment at having our hiking plans thwarted by Joaquin's arrival subsided a little as we marvelled at the magnificence of the elements against the dramatic natural landscape.

We clambered down a steep path to reach an area thick with bamboo plants, beyond which was a small beach. Every inch of this tiny cove screeched 'popular with surfers' and I don't only mean abandoned surfboards and burnt-out campfires (there were those too). Looking around, it was clear the wave worshippers who use this beach have minimal respect for dry land – or for their fellow humans who enjoy walking the coastline. This pretty, secluded cove had been transformed into an open-air sewer with soiled toilet paper and human excrement evident everywhere.

Having descended to beach level, there was now a steep climb back to the clifftop. While I huffed and puffed my way up the footpath, Harri reassured me that this would be the toughest uphill section we'd be tackling today. I didn't believe him of course. Harri utters these assurances at regular intervals for the purpose of keeping my spirits up. Later on, when we encounter a mountain of Himalayan proportions he'll pretend to study the map intensely, before raising those impressive eyebrows in mock horror. How could there be a mountain left to climb? There must be some mistake – this one definitely wasn't on the map earlier. Eventually, he'll shrug and admit he's made a gaffe, maybe failed to notice that very small zero on the end of the stated altitude. If I'm really lucky, I may just catch the tail end of a mumbled apology, but only very occasionally.

Once we were back on higher ground, there was a long section on level forestry tracks. This is the kind of terrain I fantasize about when I'm slogging up vertical hills or through soggy marshland, but quickly tire of when I'm actually walking it. Believe me, kilometre after kilometre of viewless hiking can become very tedious.

We fell into a companionable silence and I began to imagine a different kind of holiday, the kind our friends mostly opt for. In May, we stayed in Lagos for one night, and now I wondered why we couldn't have stayed in one of its narrow, historic streets for longer, enjoying good food and a twice-daily stroll along the promenade or beach. An occasionally restful break would be nice, I thought, instead of these super-active breaks that leave me in need of another holiday.

'I'd much rather be on a boat trip right now,' I mused aloud, knowing Harri would switch off the moment he heard the word 'boat' or when I mentioned any holiday proposals that didn't involve hiking. There was no answer and I knew I was wasting my breath. In his books, it's not a *proper* holiday unless we clock up at least 15 miles a day, preferably more.

We'd veered inland and wouldn't be returning to the coast until the end of today's section. We were following the Historical Way to reach Carrapateira, another favourite surfing resort. The Rota Vicentina website waxes lyrically about this section describing it thus: 'practically a step-by-step summary of what the Rota Vicentina has to offer: the power of the sea pouring over ancient cliffs or on quiet sandy beaches, undergrowths full of colour and aromas, an extraordinary biodiversity of fauna, tranquil woods of cork, wild olive and oak trees, meadows cultivated by man at his leisure, visited at night by boars and badgers, a spring which erupts in flowers and colourful insects, a fall that has mushrooms and edible wild plants, points of contemplation at sea level ... '. Wow, it was hard not be seduced by such evocative marketing spiel.

At Monte Novo, we passed a traditional farm with hens, a cockerel and several cows grazing freely near some outbuildings. Two dilapidated carts – minus the horses – had been 'parked' in front of the farmhouse. In short, it looked like a scene from a bygone age and I spent a fair few minutes getting the perfect shot of one of the hens snuggling up to the cockerel. Harri had walked off ahead and it was only when I caught up with him, he told me an old man had been sitting outside the farmhouse the whole time, presumably wondering why a middle-aged woman in shorts was taking so many photographs of his farming stock.

We'd barely left the farm behind when we spotted a strange menagerie heading in our direction. In rural Algarve, it's not unusual to see unattended herds of cattle or goats moving to new pastures; however, this was the first time we'd seen several horses in their midst. We waited, hoping they'd leave the track, but they continued moving towards us. It was only when they were almost upon us, that I spotted the bull in their midst. Now, as every hiker knows, the only sensible thing to do when confronted with an oncoming bull is to get out of its way – and fast!

Unlike yesterday, there was no twine between us and the oncoming animals. Neither was there anywhere obvious to scarper on this open landscape; the vegetation was low-lying and there wasn't a tree, or even a human-sized shrub, within the immediate vicinity. With nowhere to run or hide, our only hope was to 'convince' the bull that we didn't represent a threat to his cows. Without a minute to lose, we launched ourselves into the scrubland alongside the track. Ignoring its scratchiness against my bare legs, I put my head down, ostrich-like, and focussed on putting as much distance as possible between the bull and me. It seemed to work, because a few minutes later the convoy had passed and I could allow myself to breathe easily again.

Talking of bulls, I was surprised to learn the Spanish are not alone in having a long tradition of bull fighting. The sport – and I hesitate to call it that – remains popular in certain parts of Portugal but with one huge difference. In Spain, the *tercio de muerte* (the killing of the bull by the matador) is all part of the spectacle – albeit a rather gruesome part – while in Portugal it has been illegal to kill a bull in the ring since 1928. This law is rigorously applied to all bull fights except, bizarrely, those taking place in the little border town of Barrancos. The townsfolk here must be a bloodthirsty lot. They felt so strongly that their annual August festival just wasn't the same without a bloodied, dead bull to gawk at that for nearly a decade the town's civil leadership just ignored the ban, stuck two fingers up at animal rights' defenders, successfully fought 100 law suits, and carried on with the 'local tradition' of savaging bulls in the ring. The Mayor's bloody-mindedness (and never has a word seemed so apt) eventually paid off and in 2002, another law was passed, this time granting a special exception from the law for Barrancos.

There are other notable differences between Portuguese and Spanish bullfights. First, there is the little matter of those blunted horns, rendering a bull in Portugal less likely to do real harm to a human than their counterparts in Spain.

Secondly, bull-fighting in Portugal is more of a team effort than Spanish bullfighting, where the matador will taunt the bull single-handedly. Here, there are the cavaleiros, skilled horsemen who are trained in bullfighting and whose raison d'être is to stab the bull in the back with several small javelins. Enter the forcados, a group of eight men who further provoke and eventually subdue the huge beast with their own hands. The forcados are assisted by additional 'foot soldiers' known as bandarilheiros, whose function seems to be to provide additional spectacle/entertainment. In Spain, it is the matador who is the main man, while in Portugal the kudos goes to the cavaleiros.

Of course, it's hard to visualise how all this frenzied activity pans out without actually watching a bullfight firsthand ... something I can assure you is never going to happen. Not in Spain and not in Portugal. While Portugal's 90-year-old law against killing bulls in the rings might sound like a (long-ago) step in the right direction, the constant jabbing of bandarilhas into the animal's back is certainly not pain-free and many animals die as a result of the blood loss incurred in the ring. Even animals that get the upper hand in the ring fare no better overall as they are often killed within a few days. It seems more likely the legislation was introduced to spare the sensitivities of the audience and not out of any concern for the level of pain and distress a bull is subjected in the ring.

Happily, the popularity of bull fighting seems to be on the decline in both countries. In Spain, the Catalonian parliament voted to ban it in 2010, nearly two decades after it was outlawed in the Canary Islands.

Luckily for us, the bull on the track showed no indication of being trained for combat and barely glanced in our direction as he sauntered past. All the excitement had left us feeling a little peckish: it was time to find somewhere to settle down for a snack. In practice, this wasn't as easy as it sounded and just when we were thinking we had no choice but to plonk ourselves down on the stony ground we happened upon an abandoned whitewashed farmhouse with the familiar *Vende Se* scrawled on one of its walls.

One end of the property was dilapidated and falling down, but the other end looked as though it had been lived in relatively recently. Some small farming implements were propped against the house and the garden looked like it had been well-tended in the not-so-distance past. Harri sat on a waist-high wall lined with terracotta tiles and delved into his rucksack for food. I was intrigued by this abandoned homestead and wondered why its last residents had packed up and left. Certainly, someone had once cared very much about transforming this tranquil property into a home. There was an overgrown palm tree, lots of cacti and a curious owl statue. Whoever lived here had clearly loved the beach for they had set an assortment of sea shells among the uneven stone slabs. A little distance away a solitary pampas grass swayed in the breeze, a poignant reminder that the overgrown land had once been someone's cherished garden.

On the ground in front of the property someone had painstakingly created a five-point star from lighter-coloured stones. I pondered about the significance of this symbol. The Moors believed that painting bright blue on external walls would ward off evil spirits; it's why so many traditional properties in Algarve, including this one, display a bright blue 'trim' painted along the bottom of the walls and around the doorways. I wondered if the five-pointed star might have been created as another talisman to represent love, truth, peace, freedom and justice.

All too soon it was time to move on, which was a shame because I'd have been happy ambling around in that overgrown garden for hours. I hoped it wouldn't be too long before someone stumbled upon this peaceful property and fell in love with it. Tender, loving care was all that was needed to transform it back into a wonderful home.

For the next hour or so, we followed a level track through pine, eucalyptus and shrubs. Amber-coloured dragonflies (or perhaps damsel flies) flitted around us, tantalising me with photographic possibilities every time they landed on nearby vegetation, but ultimately moving too fast for me to have any chance of snapping them. In the end, I was trailing so far behind, I had to give up and hurry after Harri.

We crossed the main Aljezur to Carrapateira road and marvelled at how a decent (and preferably fast) road pulls in the property developers. Pretty as the setting was, the house where we'd eaten elevenses was never going to be sought-after by foreign buyers simply because there was no road access. Here, the beautiful, rolling landscape was both agricultural and easily accessible. Many old *quintas* had been renovated and now were now presented as pristine, whitewashed homes with terraced gardens and plenty of outdoor living space. Our favourite was a converted windmill. Harri thought the area was very much as he imagined rural France to look, although I suspect property prices here in rural Algarve are ever-so-slightly higher.

We'd been looking forward to a beer in Bordeira – a sleepy traditional village of the picture postcard variety – but today being Monday, the bar in question was firmly *fechado*. Wanting to be absolutely certain there wasn't a second bar/cafe doing a roaring trade around the corner, we strolled around the tiny village. Our two-minute meanderings took us to the rear house which had been 'enhanced' with some additional windows and a new back door. The open door led to an orange tree which was guarded by a dog, while one of the windows overlooked the sea. None of these fixtures or landscapes were real, you understand, but had been painted onto the property to transform what would otherwise have been a nondescript white wall into something passersby would find interesting and attractive. I love random acts of creativity like this!

Having exhausted any possibility of a beer in Bordeira, there was little point in hanging around. This Monday closing tradition can be frustrating, especially as it seems to be widely observed. When we walked the Via Algarviana, we arrived in Alte – a popular tourist town – on a Monday afternoon to find everything closed. Worse, we finished the 300km distance on a Monday, which meant were unable to fully explore the lighthouse at Cabo de São Vicente.

After hours of relatively easy walking, we now had a hill to climb … and it was going to be a steep one, Harri warned. He wasn't joking, the hill was a killer and I had to stop for several breathers; however, the reward for getting to the top was immediate. The land levelled off to reveal a small but perfectly formed lake. It was time to stop for lunch. There were no picnic benches so we settled down on the rocky shoreline – one of the advantages to hiking in a hot country is no wet bums! Here the dragonflies were large and red; they seemed in less of a flutter than their golden cousins, and were perfectly happy to be photographed.

Before long we were walking in wooded hills again. There were no distant views but with such spectacularly pretty scenery no-one was complaining. Goat farming seems to be very common in this part of Algarve; we passed an area of open land where I counted well over a hundred grazing. Eventually, we began our descent to Carrapateira following a track through a deep-sided valley with the ocean ahead.

There was a short stretch of walking along the main road – we haven't found road walking to be a huge problem in Algarve, possibly because there is so little traffic on most of the roads (except perhaps in Portimão at rush hour!) – and then we were approaching our destination. As we strolled into Carrapateira, we passed a large billboard advertising the nearby Museum of the Sea and Earth. It wasn't late and we might have passed an interesting hour or so at the museum; however this being Monday ...

Maybe it was the dark clouds gathering overhead, the cold gusts of wind, or perhaps the sprawling dune system running down to the ocean, but everything about this landscape around me reminded me of north Cornwall. From where we were standing, it looked as if several houses had been built on the sand dunes, and while they looked spectacular, I wondered about the long-term viability of such a home? Didn't the very nature of a sand dune system mean it was always shifting? So where did that leave the foundations of your house in a couple of decades? When sea levels rise, as they surely will, would you find yourself floating out to sea in your 'ark'? Or perhaps our eyes were deceiving us and the houses weren't built on sand after all.

These days Carrapateira is very much a surfing resort (the historic village is set a fair distance back from the beach). In fact, the very conditions that now attract surfers were once responsible for many shipwrecks along this stretch of coastline. In the 17th century, the area was also susceptible to raids by Barbary pirates. Local people petitioned for protection and a small fort was erected in 1673. Like so much of Portugal's built landscape, the fort was damaged in the Lisbon earthquake of 1755 and was decommissioned in the early nineteenth century.

We stopped at the Restaurante do Cabrita on the way into town for a beer and some olives, where the young male waiter's customer service skills did nothing to impress us, then set about finding our accommodation. Harri had already warned me that our room was not *en suite* and I was doing my best to be philosophical about the prospect of scuffling along the corridor in the early hours if I needed a wee. It's funny how you get used to things: an en suite bedroom would have been considered super posh twenty years ago but now they have become the norm. Fail to provide them at your peril!

In one Falmouth hotel where I stayed regularly, I remember how a bay-windowed double room was 'modernised' by building not one but two en suite facilities. On one side of the window a stud partition housed a miniscule toilet cubicle and on the other side an identical room boasted a tiny shower. The room's aesthetics were completely ruined, of course, but the hotelier was at least attempting to meet guests' insistence for *en suite* facilities. I can actually remember staying at a Penzance guesthouse where there wasn't an electric socket in my room, but that's a whole other story!

Anyway, I'd promised Harri that I wouldn't make a fuss about tonight's bathroom facilities room and I intended to keep my word.

Carrapateira is one of the most popular resorts on the western Algarve coast, mainly because of its sweeping and unspoilt beaches. To the north of the village is the wide, sandy bay formed by Praia da Bordeira, widely regarded as one of Portugal's best beaches. Further south is another beautiful sandy beach, Praia do Amado, which is more open to the Atlantic winds and extremely popular with surfers. Rugged limestone cliffs separate the two bays, and there is a waymarked walking route, the Pontal da Carrapateira Circuit.

It took us a little while to track down Carrapateira Lodge, probably because it was located one of the backstreets in the level part of town. I'd been a little nervous about what to expect, but we were greeted enthusiastically which always helps. Upstairs our room was interesting … I'm not sure if 'funky' might be the word I'm looking for. Our bed was made from pallets (nothing wrong with that) and had a sort of decorative ledge all the way around. There were white net drapes hanging over the bed (presumably to keep flies away during the summer months) and for once, the mirror was hanging at the perfect height for me. Frustratingly, there was a complete absence of chairs or other potential hanging places, making it a little impractical for hikers like us who need to do a little laundry from time to time.

So far, we appeared to be the only guests. I was relieved to see the shared bathroom with its nautical theme was directly opposite our room, but less enthusiastic about the four bedded room next to it. Six people sharing one bathroom? It might get a bit frantic at busy times ... like bedtime and before breakfast. Were guests expected to queue on the landing or pop in and out of their room at regular intervals to check if the bathroom was free? I remembered my promise and said nothing.

There was no-one else around, so we decided to have a little snoop around. One of the online reviewers had mentioned the only en suite bedroom was a little unusual in its layout and we were keen to find out what they meant. We tiptoed along the corridor and peered into the room. What looked like floor-to-ceiling fitted wardrobes lined one wall, but on closer inspection, all was not what it seemed. One of the sliding doors was slightly ajar revealing a gleaming white WC. I poked my head around the door to find an entire bathroom crammed inside the wardrobe. Someone clearly thought these compact arrangements were a genius solution to the en suite challenge, but there's no way I'd have wanted to shower in a wardrobe! Talk about claustrophobic. Far from being worried about the shared bathroom, I now felt relieved that we hadn't booked this 'en suite' room.

Back in our room, I was pondering the strange nomadic life of a backpacker, when Harri came rushing in.

'You'll never guess what I've just found,' he said. Curious, I followed him along the corridor to a closed door.

'I wondered where this door led,' he explained. 'Then I opened it and got the shock of my life.'

He turned the handle to reveal the little white face of a fluffy rabbit. The rabbit, which appeared to be living out there on the narrow balcony overlooking the street, was clearly delighted at our unexpected intrusion and even keener to escape into the corridor. Although it didn't seem at risk of falling to its death (the rails were too close together) the idea of keeping a rabbit on a tiled balcony high above the ground seemed rather cruel. Not that there was much we could do about it ... we could hardly 'rescue' the bunny and take it with us!

We had planned to eat outside one of the eateries surrounding Carrapateira's small *praça* – the burger bar is supposed to be very good – but the similarities with the Cornish coast didn't end with the landscape. The weather had taken a downturn again and the wind had whipped up to such an extent that eating *al fresco* would have required far warmer clothing than we possessed. There didn't seem to be any restaurants with indoor seating so, against our better judgement, we headed back to Restaurante do Cabrita where at least we could sit inside.

The sullen waiter's mood hadn't improved in the passing hours. Sometimes it's hard to put your finger on exactly what it is that makes someone appear rude. This young man carried out his duties efficiently enough. He took our order, brought our drinks, didn't mess up the meals ... however, there was something about his attitude, his unsmiling face, his failure to engage us in any conversation at all, that made us feel that our presence in the restaurant was unwelcome.

(I later checked the reviews on Trip Advisor, and was interested to see that a month before our visit, another customer had picked up on the waiter's frostiness and written: 'Had a lovely meal here; the fish was fresh and delicious. All the side [dishes] were lovely too. Waiter was not as welcoming as most others have been in this part of Portugal'.

I echoed those sentiments. The food was okay though nothing special, the restaurant was clean and nicely decorated, but there was definitely something missing re the usual friendly ambiance of a Portuguese restaurant. As seems to be the norm, the large-screen television was on and said waiter seemed to split his time between staring at the screen with a bored expression and staring rudely at me. But perhaps I'm just being paranoid.

Tomorrow we would be back at Vila do Bispo and, for me, that could mean only one thing – a Lidl supermarket! We could buy provisions in a friendly supermarket, cook it in the shared kitchen and eat outside under the stars. Weather permitting, of course.

For photographs visit uk.pinterest.com/thewalkerswife

DAY 8: CARRAPATEIRA TO VILA DO BISPO

The bunny on the balcony had been abandoned. Not on the balcony but in one of the guest rooms, which rather begs the question 'who in their right mind would take their pet rabbit on holiday with them?' Still, I suppose it takes all sorts. Anyway, the brother and sister who run the guesthouse had assumed responsibility for the poor creature and, as the villa didn't have any suitable outdoor space, they'd had no alternative but to create a home for it on that balcony.

It had again rained heavily during the night. As usual I hadn't heard a thing, but the downpour had kept Harri awake for a while. This morning, there was no indication the Algarve sunshine was going to put in an appearance anytime soon and my heart sank at the prospect of another overcast day. The weather has been really disappointing on this trip and I'm getting sick of people telling us how unusual it is to have this much cloud, rain and wind in early October ... well, we know who's to blame, don't we? Joaquin.

Our bed of pallets, the potentially-shared bathroom and the rabbit on the terrace were instantly forgotten when we presented ourselves for breakfast and cast our eyes on the veritable feast awaiting us: delicious homemade fruit salad, gorgeous creamy yoghurt, salame de chocolate, croissants, bread, ham, cheese ... I could go on. In fact, there was so much food set out, I wondered if a whole army of guests had arrived in the middle of the night.

We'd used the bathroom as and when we needed to without encountering a locked door or queue, which made us wonder if the pre-booked guests had even turned up. Over breakfast we learned that one other person had stayed overnight, that he was from Southampton and was here visiting his brother, a chef at nearby Casa Fajara. And what a delightful breakfast companion Ryan was. In his late twenties, he'd rejected the endless hype about work bringing fulfilment and just treated his job as a means to an end, a way of funding his passion for travel. When he wasn't hopping onto a plane to visit some distant land (or even Carrapateira) you could find him working long and unsociable hours putting out traffic cones on motorways.

This affable young man worked like mad and saved like crazy. After months of hard work, Ryan's employer was more than happy for him to take extended periods of unpaid leave to travel the world. We warmed instantly to our young companion, admiring his refreshing honestly about the reason most people go to work in the first place.

We could have stayed there chatting for longer but we needed to get a move on. We were just paying our 50 euros to the owner Catarina, when it started raining heavily again. She immediately offered us a lift. She was driving to Vila do Bispo anyway, she insisted, so we wouldn't be putting her to any trouble. Or, if we preferred, she could just transport our rucksacks to our accommodation there. Though the prospect of walking in heavy rain didn't appeal to us, we weren't ready to admit defeat and abandon our hiking plans. As for the 'rucksacks only' offer, Harri disliked the idea of being parted from any item which might prove vital at some point during the day.

We thanked Catarina for her kind offer, but explained that we'd prefer to walk, rain or no rain (I had my fingers crossed behind my back as I said this). Fortunately, she didn't seem inclined to hurry us on our way so we enjoyed a pleasant twenty minutes lingering in reception and talking about property prices in Carrapateira (unsurprisingly, they are high) and the strange incident of the rabbit on the balcony.

No matter how much longed to postpone the inevitable drenching, we couldn't stay talking to Catarina all morning. At least the rain was deliciously warm, meaning there was no need to pile on the clothes and get them all wet. Even cold-blooded *moi* was perfectly comfortable walking in light clothing, i.e. shorts, silk vest and sandals.

You can imagine how astounded we were to encounter a couple in full winter hiking gear ... full *British* winter hiking gear. Thick waterproofs over warm fleeces, knee-high boots (I kid you not) and bobble hats (okay, I made that bit up but you get the idea). In contrast, Harri and I must have looked like we'd just strolled into the hills straight from the beach ... our wet hair only adding to the illusion.

Our route out of Carrapateira had taken us directly past the now-open Museum of the Sea and Earth, although I didn't realise it at the time and wrongly assumed the glass-fronted mustard and white property on the hill was one of those architect-designed houses. I suspect Harri kept *schtum* because he knows I'll use any excuse to escape the rain. A museum tour might have proved fun too – the tour guide is a 'talking' whale called Jonas.

After a steep climb, the landscape levelled off and the walking became relatively easy. Glancing back at Bordeira beach and the drab greyness of the ocean, I was almost relieved today's walking was almost entirely inland. We meandered along the valley floor, made more scenic and lush by the recent rain.

I was slightly alarmed by a bilingual sign advising us that the route ahead was prone to flooding and to follow an alternative, higher level route during heavy rain. It *had* been raining heavily, I pointed out, but Harri shook his head. Although the route ahead would see us crossing the Carrapateira and Sinceira rivers six times, we would be fine, he insisted (why is that man *always* right?).

When Harri disappeared to the little boys' room (a dense clump of bamboo), I noticed something interesting was happening in a nearby puddle and went over to investigate.

In the UK, Flying Ants Day, as it is generally known, usually takes place in July or August when the temperature is warm enough for the ants to mate. Flying ants are just regular ants – males and the much larger queens – that develop wings so they can mate in flight.

The queen ants have a particularly adroit way of testing a potential mate's suitability; she flies away as fast as she can and if he manages to keep up with her then he's in with a chance. After mating, the ants fall to the ground. The queens lose their wings and create a nest underground and the males die. Some might survive a day or two, but once their reproductive function has been fulfilled their days are numbered. All those ants you see running around your garden are actually worker ants – and they are all female.

With equal measure of revulsion and fascination, we children would await the annual plague of the flying ants. It was always in the summer holidays, *always*. But it was now the middle of October and it seemed western Algarve was having its own Flying Ants Day. There were swarms everywhere, hitting my arms, my legs, my forehead. In the muddy water, I could see them hatching in front of my eyes.

Some unfortunates seemed to lack any sense of purpose and, rather than soaring off to participate in the mating frenzy, they dive-bombed immediately into the nearest puddle, thus qualifying for the shortest life-cycle ever.

Gradually, the weather improved and after several hours of flood-free walking, we reached Pedralva – a traditional whitewashed village with narrow cobbled streets, which has risen like a Phoenix from the ruins. Like many inland Algarve communities, Pedralva had seen its population dwindle dramatically as young people moved away to find work. By 2006, only nine people were calling the village home and the majority of properties were unfit for habitation. Like the gold-mining settlements of California, Pedralva had become a ghost town.

Thankfully, Pedralva's fortunes were transformed when it came to the attention of a Lisbon businessman called Antonio Ferreira who was looking for a holiday home in Algarve. Instead of settling upon one traditional whitewashed property, he ended up buying two – and after encouraging four colleagues to get involved in the €4 million venture – practically the entire village. At first people thought Antonio was crazy but, determined to push ahead with his vision for Pedralva, he moved his family to the village and persuaded the council to invest in the necessary infrastructure, e.g. electricity, pavements, roads, etc.

One of the hardest things proved to be tracking down the absent owners of the abandoned houses, but Antonio persevered and after eighteen months Pedralva's transformation was underway. When we walked along the narrow tiled streets, there was little evidence that this village had been dying on its feet just a decade ago. To his credit, Antonio's vision was always to roll the clock back and attract people back to Pedralva by breathing new life into the village rather than overdeveloping the place in the name of progress.

It's fair to say he's done a grand job. The houses we passed were spic and span, and several had seating outside – in one instance, bundles of hay. While the village wasn't exactly brimming with life in the middle of this October day, it was easy to imagine enjoying a great night out here against the background of reggae music. Because someone here clearly liked Bob Marley ... a lot!

We stopped for a quick beer in the beautifully refurbished bar restaurant (Sitio da Pedralva) with its white walls and brightly coloured shutters and chairs. I was intrigued by a tree which looked to be growing through the ceiling. Anticipating visitors' curiosity, Antonio had put before and after photographs of the village on the walls.

We resisted the temptations of the restaurant menu and ate our picnic lunch on a nearby bench, reluctant to leave this charming place. The long-term hope is that Pedralva will attract both outdoor and cultural/arty types. You can even get married here, though maybe I should keep quiet about that if I hope to get Harri to come here again!

Humming various Bob Marley tunes, we gave ourselves a metaphoric kick on the backside and got busy strapping on our rucksacks. We'd have been quite happy lingering on the outskirts of Pedralva listening to distant reggae tunes in the sunshine; however, we had booked a room in Vila do Bispo and needed to get a move on.

Antonio's passion for restoration is clearly catching because we were soon passing more lovingly restored properties. It never pays to get complacent though, and just as we were thinking what a wonderfully peaceful area this was, we arrived at a sprawling farmhouse where two ferocious-looking dogs were keeping guard. Happily, they were tethered, but their furious barking left us in no doubt that they'd happily sink their fangs into our legs given the chance.

Feeling weary after our prolonged beer stop, I struggled with the initial climb through eucalyptus woods. Eventually the terrain levelled off and we found ourselves wandering through a land of whirling white giants.

Wind turbines are a common enough sight here in the Algarve, a testament to Portugal's commitment to renewable energy generally, and specifically the country's focus on wind power development. In May 2016, Portugal produced all its electricity from renewable sources for a period of four days, the first European country to achieve this.

After more than a decade of hiking together in Wales, Madeira, Portugal and Spain, these towering structures have a comforting familiarity for Harri and me. In the early days of wind power, much was made about the level of noise created by the revolving rotor blades by outspoken NIMBY types, yet I cannot think of one time when we've been walking past a wind farm and had to stop talking because we couldn't hear each other (which is definitely not the case with road traffic, trains and barking dogs). Personally, I love wind turbines and enjoy walking between these imposing structures.

There were a few miles of walking on undulating dried-mud tracks through scrubby vegetation then more forestry before Vila do Bispo's distinctive water tower was visible in the distance. When hiking the Via

Algarviana we approached the town from the east via Raposeira; however, this time we were heading south along the Rota Vicentina.

We had decided to stay at the same hotel as last time (Casa Mestre) – we'd liked it very much and it was inexpensive. When we rolled up outside the large property, however, it was unrecognisable. Since our last visit, the exterior had undergone a complete makeover and now the hotel that overlooked Vila do Bispo's lively praça looked very elegant and upmarket indeed (fortunately, this uplift was not reflected in the prices).

The property was built in 1938 for Jose Mestre Revez, the largest grain producer in the region south of the Tagus River, suggesting that it had once welcomed far more illustrious guests than Harri and me.

I always experience a pang of disappointment when we return to a much-loved hotel or restaurant for a second or third visit and experience not even a glimmer of recognition from the employees and/or management. Of course, the nature of tourism means they are welcoming new guests to the establishment all the time, and will only ever remember the odd few visitors (probably the most disagreeable ones). On the other hand, it's human nature to *want* to be remembered ... we all consider ourselves to be unique, after all. Alas, it was not to be. In the five months since our last visit, Harri and I had been forgotten.

Our double room overlooked the hotel's delightful courtyard and was even nicer than last time, with parquet flooring, wooden shutters and cane furniture. It was also conveniently located opposite the shared kitchen. After days of inclement weather, the sunshine had finally returned with the promise of a beautiful evening. We'd eaten at a local restaurant last time we were here, but tonight we intended to cook for ourselves and make the most of that gorgeous courtyard.

As any chef will confirm, it takes considerable culinary ingenuity to create a tasty meal without access to olive oil, spices and herbs, or salt and pepper. I've only once stayed in self-catering accommodation where the owner provided holidaymakers with a store cupboard of standard spices, herbs and condiments (in Barcelona). The standard set-up in most places is to provide crockery, pots and pans, but nothing more. Casa Mestre was no different and, although the kitchen was well-equipped, I would need to be creative with my cooking.

Thankfully, there was a Lidl supermarket a ten-minute walk away. We filled our trolley with fresh pasta, ham, butter, croissants (for the morning) and olives, then added lager and, at the last minute, a bottle of *vinho verde* for just €3.29.

Harri hadn't been feeling 100% since Arrifana, so I left him lying on the bed writing up notes for his guidebook about hiking the Via Algarviana while I pottered around the kitchen, careful to avoid whacking my head on the huge chimney above the cooker.

When it was ready, we carried our meal outside to the large table closest to the kitchen and were slightly taken aback to see another guest had beaten us to it. It would have been churlish to head across the courtyard and sit separately at an even bigger table next to the barbecue area, so we asked the man sitting there if minded us joining him.

Cameron seemed pleased to have our company. He told us he knew the area well and was learning Portuguese. He used to be a keen sea swimmer who thought nothing of swimming a mile out to sea until a freak accident injured his big toe so badly it effectively put an end to his open air swimming. I shuddered, imagining an encounter with a shark or thinking he'd somehow got embroiled in fishing net, but I was way-off. It transpired that Cameron's accident had not happened at sea at all, but on the beach at Sagres.

He'd been strolling along the sand directly below high, limestone cliffs when a piece of rock fell from above and landed on his shoe, cutting straight through the fabric and severing his big toe. Fortunately, the good people of Sagres had rushed to help, he received emergency first aid there on the beach and his toe was subsequently successfully reconnected to his foot.

Our new Scottish friend recounted this anecdote with good humour, in that 'you win some, you lose some' kind of way (in this instance 'it' being his big toe that was almost lost). He realised he'd been lucky. Sadly, despite all the best efforts of the authorities, the crumbling cliffs of Algarve claim far too many lives. In August 2009, a Portuguese family of four was killed in a landslide on Maria Luisa beach in Albufeira (another person lost their life in the same accident).

As this rather gruesome conversation took place while we were eating, I was relieved we were eating pasta and not steak!

For photographs visit uk.pinterest.com/thewalkerswife

DAY 9: VILA DO BISPO TO CABO DE SÃO VICENTE

'I have a proposal for you,' Harri called out from the shower.
After nearly a decade together, I guessed he wasn't about to ask me to marry him.

I was right. What he was proposing was a change of itinerary, which considering how much time he spends planning our hiking trips beforehand, was probably as much of a shock as if he had actually proposed marriage.

Rather than spend our last day in Portugal walking from Lagos to Bensafrim and back again – as originally intended – he wondered if I might prefer to rest my legs and linger awhile in Lagos? Would I heck? We spent a night in Lagos after completing the Via Algarviana and I'd loved the city from the moment we stepped off the bus into the strong gusts coming off the Bensafrim river. On that occasion, we'd had insufficient time to explore the city fully, a fact we both lamented. Even so, suggesting we abandon an out-and-back hike in favour of a couple of days of sightseeing was so out of character that I wondered if Harri had whacked his head on the shower head (or had another encounter with a bidet).

Before he had time to change his mind – and determined to hold him to his word – I shouted back 'yes'. As far as I was concerned, the longer we had to chill out in Lagos the better.

There are two waymarked routes to Cabo de São Vicente from Vila do Bispo: the Via Algarviana (GR13), which we followed when we completed the full 300km trail, and the Rota Vicentina (GR11) which we planned to follow today. The GR11 heads west, reaching the coast at Torre de Aspa before heading south to the finish along the Fishermen's Trail. To further complicate matters, there is another route choice to make when you reach Ponta Ruiva. The GR11 continues on tracks and lanes across the flat coastal plain while the Fishermen's Trail is a more demanding clifftop route past the Telheiro beach. Both GR11 routes rejoin just north of Cabo de São Vicente (together with the Via Algarviana). Same end destination, just a different way of getting there.

Yesterday's route had taken us inland and away from the ocean, so we opted to follow the tougher coastal option today. The weather seemed to be on our side once more. After days of grey skies and intermittent rain, Algarve's famous wall-to-wall sunshine was back. We had gone to bed far later than customary last night – with the result that neither of us wanted to leap out of bed at dawn. Thankfully, there was no dining room to report to at a set time, just some croissants, yoghurt and mango juice from Lidl.

Before we left Casa Mestre, I couldn't resist one last stroll around the courtyard. This beautiful property is so deceptive from the street. It's not until you step inside you realise how sprawling the place is with its little annexes and outbuildings scattered all over the place. In the courtyard, there are doors and steps everywhere, leading onto various terraces and seating areas. From high walls and shadowy corners, cats peered out at us; last night we'd watched in amazement as one of the resident moggies scrambled squirrel-like up the wooden pole opposite our window.

There are many succulents and tropical plants growing here, including what looked like banana plants. For the umpteenth time, I thought how wonderful it must be to live in such gloriously lush surroundings.

We left Vila do Bispo on an undulating road across the relatively flat coastal plain passing many traditional homesteads with small patches of land. We guessed these were the kind of properties Catarina had in mind when she'd told us housing on the outskirts of Vila do Bispo was more affordable than the more sought-after properties of Carrapateira.

The road gradually turned into a wide dirt track with forestry to our right. This was easy, flat walking and we covered several kilometres very quickly. Vehicle after vehicle passed with surfing boards strapped to their roofs. Eventually, we left the forest behind and the landscape opened out in all directions. Without a hedge in sight, we could see for miles.

I was casting my eyes around for the next set of green and turquoise stripes (thus confirming that we hadn't strayed from the route) when Harri dropped his bombshell.

'I didn't want to alarm you,' he said, 'but in an hour or so, we'll be coming to a ravine and the only way of crossing it is to drop into it by means of a ladder.'

Ravine? This was the first I'd heard of a ravine.

The 60-kilometre stretch of imposing dark shale and greywacke cliffs between Odeceixe in the north and Vila do Bispo in the south is called the Costa Vicentina, hence the Rota Vicentina. Some of those cliffs tower 50 metres above sea level and we'd already witnessed the power of the waves crashing against them. I pictured a ravine of *Indiana Jones'* proportions. One foot wrong and we'd be plummeting into the Atlantic Ocean.

'Why ... why didn't you mention this before?' I demanded.

'After you froze on that footpath near Poio, I thought I'd better not mention it until the last-minute,' he said.

Harri's logic baffled me. He'd witnessed just how terrified I'd been on that cliff edge, yet still thought I'd be up for some ravine climbing? How would not warning me about the danger in advance stop me being scared? I hadn't known about the collapsed footpath near Poio until it disappeared in front of me and that episode nearly ended badly.

I knew the real reason he'd kept quiet about the imminent ravine. If I'd known about it from the outset, I'd have tried to dissuade him from following this route. Too right he knew that dangling over a ravine on a rope ladder was not high up there on my bucket list.

Resisting the urge to throw something at him – we both knew there was an alternative route to Cabo de São Vicente because we'd walked it in May – I searched desperately for my inner lion, telling myself that I used to be okay with heights in Madeira. Okay, perhaps not okay, but *okayish*. Some of those high-level levada walks could be pretty hairy at times, but when we'd encountered unprotected sections of footpath with big drops, I'd coped with my vertigo by walking inside the levada, getting my feet wet if necessary.

For the next hour, I alternated between false cheeriness (of the 'what can be better than walking along the clifftops in warm sunshine?' kind) and overwhelming panic. That this popular coastal footpath – the GR11 no less – had allowed a ravine to develop on its route made me cross. It was the same sense of injustice I experienced upon discovering a field I regularly walked/ran through was suddenly and inexplicably populated by a herd of bullocks.

'Just wait and see,' Harri called back, when he noticed I was dragging my feet and falling behind. 'You never know, you might be working yourself up for nothing.'

'Huh.'

I swear I'd have tossed his sandwiches into the sea had Harri had the gall to say 'I told you so' when we finally reached the Quebradas ravine. Even I had to admit the 'ravine' was pretty tame by geological standards, and rather than being a frayed rope affair, the ladder was sturdy and short. Short, because the ravine was shallow and not at all scary, even for a wuss like me. I'd spent the past hour or so imagining I'd be dangling from some rope ladder high above the waves and all I had to do was climb carefully down five wooden steps onto what was unquestionably solid ground. What an idiot!

This wild and windswept coastline, from Porto Covo in the Alentejo to Burgau on the southern Algarve coast, forms the Parque Natural do Sudoeste Alentejano e Costa Vicentina, an area of protected status. Salty winds batter this exposed landscape at speeds of up to 100 kilometres an hour. No trees grow here, just shrubby low-level vegetation which clings to the exposed cliffs. Algarve springtime is well underway by February/March, when these clifftops are transformed into a wild garden of pink, red, purple, yellow and white blooms, including many rare wild orchids. The shrubby violet grows along the roadside, its only other natural habit being Cape Trafalgar in southern Spain, and the scent of wild thyme fills the air.

Now it was autumn and the colours were less vivid. Instead, our eyes were drawn to the turquoise waters far below. Without venturing too close to the cliff edge, it was difficult to catch a glimpse of the small sandy coves lying along their base, but it was enough to know they were there, timeless and unspoilt.

We had emerged from the ravine and were following a steep footpath along a particularly stunning stretch of coast when I spotted the biggest beetle I'd ever seen shuttling along on the dusty ground. I'm far from being an entophile, but I do find myself glancing at the floor a lot when I'm hiking just to avoid accidentally standing on anything that might be living at ground level. Stepping on the occasional ant or little creature is probably unavoidable; however, I would never stand on an insect deliberately, not even a spider. Not if I spotted it first.

It would have been impossible not to notice this specimen. With hindsight, we think it might have been a European stag beetle. The largest beetle on the continent is now classified as Near Threatened in the International Union for Conservation of Nature's Red List, in the main because the species has lost much of its oak wood habitat. So concerned are naturalists that this giant-sized beetle is heading the way of the dodo that thirteen European counties, including Portugal and the UK, belong to the European Stag Beetle Monitoring Network, established to learn more about the insect's population size and distribution and to identify trends. In 2016, Portugal's first annual survey revealed between 470 and 550 stag beetle observations during June and July, all of them north of Lisbon. The insects were not only found in woodland (their natural habitat) but also in houses, alongside roads and in urban parks.

Finding one here in western Algarve didn't necessarily mean we had the wrong species, just that there were no observers working in this region or even that the observers weren't particularly observant.

A British stag beetle enthusiast called Maria Fremlin has created a hugely informative website about this fascinating family of insects who spend the majority of their lives (three to four years) inside dead wood. And if you're in any doubt that Ms Fremlin really loves stag beetles, the heading on her site's home page reads 'Stag beetles – all they need is love and wood'. When stag beetles finally emerge from the wood it is with the sole purpose of finding a female to mate with, dead or alive. Yep, male stag beetles have been known to cosy up to deceased females who are still emitting sex pheromones. We'll never know if the female (it was lacking the huge mandibles of a male) on the footpath was a European stag beetle or not, but I'm so relieved I glanced down before I plunged my foot to the ground and crushed it.

Unfortunately, even empty clifftops can attract top-class idiots and the delightful tranquillity of our Algarvian idyll was suddenly shattered by a shrill voice. Just a few moments earlier, we'd exchanged a genial bom dia with a young shepherd leaning on his crook and enjoying the sunshine, surrounded by his large herd of cattle and goats. He was assisted in his role by no fewer than five dogs, who seemed more interested in keeping an eye on us than the herd.

Harri and I are not dog owners. We probably never will be, not because we don't like dogs. I quite fancy the idea of having a sausage dog poking its nose out of my handbag ... *I'm only joking,* for me it would have to be an energetic breed, like a Border Collie, a Red Setter or a Dalmatian. No, the reason we have repeated ignored well-meaning friends' suggestions that we should join the dog-owning fraternity (*'you two really should get a dog, all that walking you do'*) is because our four-legged friends can be a real liability when you're hiking in the UK. There, at least, there are generally field boundaries (hedging, fencing, ditches, barbed wire, etc) to prevent an undisciplined mutt charging at farming stock. Here on the windswept cliffs of the Parque Natural do Sudoeste Alentejano e Costa Vicentina the land was open and the cows and goats roamed as freely as they'd always done. If any one of them had even considered making a dash for freedom, their ankle-nipping guards were always one step ahead.

On hearing the woman's shouts, *everyone* – Harri, the shepherd and me – immediately turned our heads to see what was wrong. And what *was* wrong was that her Border Collie was charging straight at the herd, causing such panic among the goats that they were now rushing onto the dirt track and blocking our way.

We were bemused by the shepherd's nonchalant attitude towards the ensuing chaos until we realised that, in its enthusiasm to chase the herd, the woman's pet had failed to register that it was not the only dog in these parts. In fact, there were now five sets of menacing teeth advancing towards it. Talk about a quick retreat. Having ignored its owner's original shouts, the collie now did the fastest about-turn in history and galloped back to the safety of her legs. The shepherd twisted around on his crook and his dogs sloped back to his side, satisfied with a job well done.

Now the track on the stony, sandy ground became less clear and we were guided across the scrub by a series of small stone cairns and splashes of paint, which were easy to miss. Fortunately, we couldn't go far wrong when our end destination – the lighthouse at Cabo de São Vicente – loomed large and loud on the headland. After a very rocky section, we rejoined the route of the Historical Way and Via Algarviana behind a spectacular crescent-shaped bay.

The plan had always been to catch the 3.05pm bus to Lagos, but we arrived with plenty of time to kill – more time than was needed to grab a beer and eat our picnic lunch – so we headed past the umpteen souvenir and gift stalls stretching along the roadside. If we'd been surprised by the crowds on our last visit, this time around it was like dodging traffic in Manhattan. Car doors were being flung open alongside *and into* us, while reckless drivers making last-minute swerves into roadside spaces ignored anyone in their path. It was essential to keep our wits about us if we wanted to reach the lighthouse in one piece.

Our customary naff timing meant we'd finished walking the Via Algarviana on a Monday, the day many of Portugal's museums and tourist attractions are closed. This meant we'd been unable to pass beyond the tall boundary walls and had no choice but to snap our 'finish' photographs in front of locked gates. On this second visit, we were delighted to find everything was not only open but that entrance was free (although we soon realised the astronomic prices in the gift shop made up for any lost revenue – a normal sized bag of coconut macaroons cost an unbelievable €8.70).

Funnily enough, Kate (Arrifana Retreat) had been bemoaning Portugal's love of issuing tickets, but this was the first time we had firsthand experience. Going to the toilet required first queuing in the foyer to purchase a ticket for 50 cents and then queuing again to gain entry to the cubicles using said ticket. Plan your call of nature well ahead in the busy summer months, ladies and gentlemen.

Inside the walls, there was a museum, a bar, plenty of viewpoints and an Alice in Wonderland seat for tourists to clamber onto and pose for photographs. We took turns taking photographs with some American tourists who hailed from Austin, Texas so we now have the cheesiest photograph of us at the end of the Via Algarviana, even if it wasn't taken when we actually finished walking the trail. We stood around for a while afterwards, incredulous at the humiliating antics our fellow tourists were prepared to endure to get onto that chair. As relatively nimble hikers, Harri and I had scrambled onto the huge seat without any problem, but not everyone was finding it so easy. We watched with uneasy fascination as large bottoms were pushed and shoved and eventually heaved into position. Oh, the indignity of it all.

It was certainly hard to equate this crazy tourist-filled location with the once-sacred spot where people thought the world ended and the sun sank into the ocean (the cape's spectacular sunsets still draw huge crowds on cloudless evenings). The first primitive lighthouse was cared for by a group of Franciscan friars living on the cape and was only replaced by the present lighthouse – one of the most powerful in Europe – in 1846.

I often wonder what it is that fuels our endless fascination with 'extreme' promontories of land? Headlands, capes, peninsulas ... call them what you will, but even in this modern age of technology and computers, they pull in the visitors by the busload. In truth, these locations just happen to jut into the ocean slightly more in whatever direction than the surrounding land. Cabo de São Vicente is not the most southerly or most westerly of mainland Portugal but the most south-westerly. The honours for the first two extreme points go to Cabo de Santa Maria and Cabo da Roca (which is also the most westerly point of mainland Europe) respectively.

So what exactly it is that makes tourists flock here in their thousands ... as they do to Land's End in Cornwall, John o' Groats in Scotland and Punta de Tarifa in Spain (the southernmost point of continental Europe where you can see Africa across the Strait of Gibraltar)? What is it about standing on these extreme promontories that so excites us all that we arrive in hoards, willingly queuing for parking spaces and waiting in line to be fleeced by opportunistic businesses?

In Madeira it's Ponta de São Lourenço on the far eastern tip of the island which draws the tourists like bees to a honey pot. Venture there and you'll find lines of people (sometimes in the flimsiest of footwear) edging their way along the often vertiginous path. But at least you can take your own photographs at Portuguese landmarks. When my youngest daughter and I visited the southernmost point of continental USA (on Key West at the tip of the Florida Keys), tourists were paying to have their photograph taken next to a large buoy-shaped monument. I hope things have changed since March 2004, but back then, a large woman 'guarded' the monument as if it was her own and insisted we paid her a dollar to take a photograph of us with our own camera.

On Wikipedia there is an entry for extreme points of earth, which – given that the earth is spherical – seems illogical until you realise the extreme compass points quoted are based on latitude and longitude, or are by continent and country.

Of course, extreme points are only truly exciting when they are located at the ocean's edge, places where the unimaginative can gather *en masse* and gaze contemplatively at the waves before heading to the nearest souvenir shop to buy the obligatory tea towel. Does anyone flock to Felsőszölnök, the westernmost point of Hungary, to stare at the trees? The camera-snapping crowds were certainly noticeable for their absence when we were walking in Lady Park Wood, near Monmouth, a few months ago. The fact that this pretty spot on the bank of River Wye marks the most easterly point of Wales seems to have escaped most people.

Neither is a fascination for bits of land that stick out into the sea a new phenomenon. Land's End in Cornwall was named Penwith Steort in 997 (Penwith is Cornish for 'extreme end' and Steort means 'tail' or 'end' in Old English).

We were rapidly tiring of the madding crowds and constant flow of traffic; it was time to go in search of solitude. Harri had earlier commented on how the sea mist was obscuring the horizon. While we'd wandering about, it had crept ever closer and had now reached headland. First the lighthouse disappeared, then the cliff edge become engulfed in mist. For the second time, our arrival at the coast had been marred with a downturn in the weather; however, it would have been foolhardy to stray too far from the road when visibility was this bad.

In the whiteout, our surroundings took on an eery silence. We bought two lagers from a burger van and settled down with our picnic on some boulders just off the road. Before long, we realised we were not alone. We had inadvertently settled down close to a pack of dogs, which appeared to be living wild on the clifftops. While they might have been wild in terms of not having owners, these thin, nervous creatures were certainly not frightening ... in fact, they seemed more afraid of us. One was curious and drifted a little closer. Seeing its pitiful condition, Harri tore off a piece of bread and tossed to the animal; however, whether it was fear or not, animal remained where it was.

We sat there a while in the swirling mist, pleased to have completed another long-distance walk in Algarve, yet reluctant to hang our trail shoes up and return to the UK. There is something wonderfully simplistic about walking every day, meeting new people and seeing different places each day.

I had a feeling this wouldn't be our last hiking trip to Algarve. *Adeus.*

For photographs visit uk.pinterest.com/thewalkerswife

USEFUL WEBSITES

The Via Algarviana (www.viaalgarviana.org)
The Rota Vicentina (en.rotavicentina.com)
Almargem (almargem.org)
Walk Algarve (www.walkalgarve.com)
Portuguese trails (www.portuguesetrails.com)
Algarve Walking Experience (www.algarvewalkingexperience.com)
Algarve Wildlife (www.algarvewildlife.com)
Hiking in Portugal (wiportugal.org)
Portugal walks (portugalwalks.com)
Tours and Tracks Algarve (www.toursandtracksalgarve.com)

Algarve Bus (information about buses and train) (www.algarvebus.info)
Comboios de Portugal (train travel) (www.cp.pt/passageiros/pt)

Algarve Tourist (www.algarve-tourist.com)
Visit Algarve (www.visitalgarve.pt)
Enjoy the Algarve (www.enjoythealgarve.com)
Algarve Uncovered (www.algarveuncovered.com)
Algarve Daily News (algarvedailynews.com)

São Marcos da Serra – discover a different Algarve
(www.saomarcosdaserra.com)
Algarve History Association (www.algarvehistoryassociation.com)

Visit Portugal (www.visitportugal.com)
Countries and their cultures
(www.everyculture.com/No-Sa/Portugal.html)
Life Cooler: Portugal is cool (en.lifecooler.com)
Portugal News (www.theportugalnews.com)
Portugal Resident (portugalresident.com)

ADDITIONAL READING

The Walkers Wife (thewalkerswife.co.uk)
Algarve Blog (algarveblog.net)
Algarve News Watch (algarvenewswatch.blogspot.pt)
It caught my eye in Portugal (delightsofthealgarve.com)
A house in the Algarve (ahouseinthealgarve.com)
Gardening in the Algarve (gardeninginthealgarve.wordpress.com)
Lisaselvidge (lisaselvidge.net)
Tom's Place (cubsur51.wordpress.com)

Sketches from Via Algarviana (Pedro M B Cabral)
Guide to the Cultural Heritage of the Algarve (free download at
www.carvoeiro.com)
A Traveller's History of Portugal (Ian Robertson)
Portugal and the Algarve: Now and Then (Jenny Grainer)
People in a Place Apart (Len Port)

OUR ACCOMMODATION

Loulé: Loulé Jardim Hotel (www.loulejardimhotel.com)
Salir: Casa da Mãe (www.casadamae.com)
Portimão: Made Inn (www.madeinn.com.pt)
Monchique: Miradoura da Serra (www.booking.com)
Aljezur: Vicentina Aparthotel (www.vicentina-aparthotel.com)
Arrifana: Arrifana Retreat (www.arrifanaretreat.com)
Carrapateira: Carrapateira Lodge (www.booking.com)
Vila do Bispo: Casa Mestre Guesthouse (www.mestreguesthouse.com)

Never Too Old To Backpack: a 364-mile walk through Wales

'Predictably, the hills were alive with Duke of Edinburgh participants. I reprimanded Harri when he groaned alongside me. These were our future customers, young people who venture into the wilderness for the first time while still in their teens and resolve to spend the rest of their lives in hiking boots. Only the majority of this lot looked pretty miserable under the weight of their huge rucksacks; worse, despite having barely left their valley campsite, they were huddling together in that all too familiar way. They couldn't be lost already, Harri sighed.'

Never too old to backpack: a 364-mile walk through Wales is a personal account of our experience of walking the undulating and frequently mountainous 23-day route from Holyhead to Chepstow devised by Harri Roberts.

From a sleepless night on a Bronze Age settlement to meltdown in Llandovery, a hunt for a long-lost friend in Beddgelert to karaoke in Brecon, Tracy shares the very best (and worst) that Wales – and long-distance hiking – has to offer.

The route was devised by Harri, who has published a separate guidebook *O Fôn i Fynwy: Walking Wales from end to end* with detailed hiking directions.

For photographs visit uk.pinterest.com/thewalkerswife

O Fôn i Fynwy: walking Wales from end to end

'In deciding upon a walking route across Wales, I was guided by the principle that the paths chosen should be walkable without undue difficulty or danger in all but the most extreme weather conditions. The basis for this decision was that one cannot choose what weather to walk in on a long-distance hike, and I didn't want to force users of this guide on to high mountaintops in unsuitable conditions. For this reason, the main route described avoids the highest summits of Snowdonia and mid-Wales, but without, I hope, sacrificing the scenic quality of these areas. In fine weather, experienced walkers are encouraged to take in as many summits as possible, and I have outlined alternative high-level routes across the Carneddau and Moel Siabod, as well as potential detours to the summits of Snowdon, Cnicht, Cadair Idris and Pumlumon.'

This 364-mile route through Wales takes its inspiration from the traditional Welsh expression 'O Fôn i Fynwy', which literally means 'from Anglesey [Ynys Môn] to Monmouthshire', but is also used to mean the whole of Wales.

This guidebook gives detailed instructions on how to follow the undulating and frequently mountainous route from Holyhead to Chepstow, with details of maps, accommodation and refreshments included.

O Fôn i Fynwy: Walking Wales from end to end' by Harri Garrod Roberts is available from Amazon's Kindle Store.

For photographs visit uk.pinterest.com/thewalkerswife

The Via Algarviana: walking 300km across the Algarve

'It must be human nature to find something to worry about, however, because no sooner had I leapt out of bed than I started to fret about the Ribeira da Foupana. Not that I was actually worried about the river – I'm sure it'll be flowing long after my own mortal soul leaves this world – but Harri had mentioned that this was one of the few Algarve rivers on our route which might pose difficulties in getting across. Almargem's Via Algarviana guide actually used the words 'an adventure' to describe crossing the Foupana, adding that the river was 'the most imposing river all along the route and that in times of heavy rain may become very dangerous or even impassable'. I didn't like the sound of that. Imposing? Did that mean the river was wide, or deep or fast-flowing? And what did they mean by dangerous? My imagination was now in overdrive.'

One week after completing the London marathon (her first), the author embarks on a long-distance backpacking trip across southern Portugal with Harri. She is confident she's fit enough to tackle the 300 kilometre Via Algarviana trail, but how will she cope when the temperature soars, no-one speaks English and drinking water is in short supply?

Follow Tracy as she hikes the tough, undulating route through depopulated villages and the beautiful mountains of inland Algarve, and gradually succumbs to the charms of a region that remains off the beaten track despite being so close to popular sandy beaches.

Away from the bustling resorts, the couple spent their days discovering a varied landscape of rolling hills, dry orchards, cork forests, and agricultural terraces. In the evenings, they enjoyed village life, traditional cuisine and the extraordinary kindness and hospitality of local people.

The Via Algarviana: walking 300km across the Algarve by Tracy Burton is available from Amazon as a paperback and an ebook.

For photographs visit <u>uk.pinterest.com/thewalkerswife</u>

The Via Algarviana: an English guide to the 'Algarve Way'

'Threading its way through the hills from settlement to settlement is the Via Algarviana ('Algarve Way'), a waymarked, long-distance trail stretching the entire length of the Algarve, from the Spanish border in the east to the Atlantic Ocean in the west. The 300km (186-mile) journey along this trail is an unforgettable experience and provides an introduction to an Algarve that few visitors ever get to see. This book describes the complete route from Alcoutim to Cabo de São Vicente (Cape St Vincent), as well as an alternative finish to the walk via Aljezur and the Rota Vicentina – another long-distance trail exploring southern Portugal's windswept Atlantic coast.'

Harri's guidebook also contains practical information for those who are contemplating walking the route, including when to go, how to get to the start at Alcoutim and the potential dangers en route.

The Via Algarviana: an English guide to the 'Algarve Way' by Harri Garrod Roberts is available from Amazon's Kindle Store.

For photographs visit uk.pinterest.com/thewalkerswife

OTHER BOOKS BY HARRI GARROD ROBERTS

Print books

Day Walks in the Brecon Beacons

Carmarthen Bay & Gower: Circular Walks along the Wales Coast Path

Carmarthenshire & Gower: Wales Coast Path Official Guide (Tenby to Swansea)

Day Walks in Pembrokeshire Coast National Park (out in spring 2018)

Digital books

Circular Walks on the Gower Peninsula

Dylan's Welsh Walks

England Coast Path: Severn Estuary & Bridgwater Bay

Castle Walks in Monmouthshire

Castle Walks in the Marches of Gwent

Castle Walks around Newport and Cardiff Rhymney Valley Walks

For more information visit thewalkerswife.co.uk